Scottish Creative Writing

Working WORDS

VALERIE THORNTON

Hodder & Stoughton
A MEMBER OF THE HODDER HEADLINE GROUP

British Library Cataloguing in Publication Data

Thornton, Valerie
  Working Words: Scottish Creative Writing
  I. Title
  820.809411

  ISBN 0-340-61870-1

First published 1995
Impression number   10 9 8 7 6 5 4 3 2 1
Year   1999 1998 1997 1996   1995

Typeset by Rowland Phototypesetting Limited, Bury St Edmunds, Suffolk.
Printed and bound in Great Britain for Hodder and Stoughton Educational, a division of
Hodder Headline Plc, 338 Euston Road, London NW1 3BH by Redwood Books,
Trowbridge.

CONTENTS

ACKNOWLEDGMENTS

I would like to thank all the writers included here for their support and willingness to be part of this book.

I would also like to thank Tommy Burns and Anniesland College in Glasgow for allowing me to use their photocopier at a crucial stage – and John Mitchell, without whose encouragement this book would not exist.

I am also very grateful to all the members of my classes, past and present, in schools and in workshops, whose working with words is a continuing source of pride and inspiration for me.

For permission to reproduce copyright material, I would like to thank the following publishers: Chatto & Windus for permission to reproduce 'Compare and Contrast' and 'Little Boy Blue' by Norman MacCaig from *Collected Poems*; also for permission to reproduce 'The Scottish National Cushion Survey' by Robert Crawford from *A Scottish Assembly*; Jonathan Cape for 'Getting Sent For' by Agnes Owens from *Lean Tales*; The Blackstaff Press for 'The Miraculous Candidate' by Bernard MacLaverty from *Secrets and Other Stories*; Canongate Press for 'The Old Woman's Reel' by Valerie Gillies from *The Chanter's Tune*; Martin Secker & Warburg for 'two fragments' by Janice Galloway from *Blood*; 'Joy' is reprinted by permission of Bloodaxe Books Ltd from *The Concrete Garden* (1991) by G. F. Dutton; HarperCollins Publishers Ltd for 'The Travelling Poet' by Iain Crichton Smith and 'Scarab' by Ian Rankin, both from *Scottish Short Stories 1986*; Chapman Publications (and Joy Hendry) for 'The Sedated' by Gordon Meade from *Singing Seals*; Carcanet Press Limited for 'Little Blue Blue' by Edwin Morgan from *Collected Poems*.

I would also like to thank the following authors for permission to reproduce copyright material: Brian McCabe for 'In the Skip' from *One Atom to Another* (Polygon, 1987); Daniel O'Rourke for 'Clockwork'; Elissa Soave for 'Hollow' from *New Writing Scotland 8* (Association for Scottish Literary Studies, 1990);

Helen Lamb for 'Solitude' and Alison Kermack for 'A Wee Tatty', both from *Original Prints Four* (Polygon, 1992); Moira Burgess for 'Surrogate' from *New Writing Scotland 3* (Association for Scottish Literary Studies, 1985); David Kinloch for 'Second Infancy' from *Paris–Forfar* (Polygon, 1994); John Glenday for 'The Apple Ghost' from *The Apple Ghost and Other Poems* (Peterloo Poets, 1989).

I am also very grateful to the following photographers: Gunnie Moberg for her permission to reproduce her photograph of Bernard MacLaverty; Fay Godwin for her photograph of Iain Crichton Smith; Alan Young for his photograph of Edwin Morgan. A final thank you goes to Robert Burns for his kindness and generosity, and for allowing me to use his photograph of Norman MacCaig.

Valerie Thornton

INTRODUCTION

The purpose of this book is to teach creative writing skills and ways of thinking creatively. It aims to show pupils in S4 to S6 how writers work. This insight will help all students who are working on creative writing assignments.

The book is in two interconnected parts: the first part explains the practical side of creative writing, exploring areas such as theme, characterisation, prose and poetic logic, and symbolism. The second part consists of nineteen texts – twelve poems and seven short stories – each of which is followed by questions and thinking points (responses to these can be prepared by groups or individuals, verbally or in writing); a piece by each author explaining how he or she came to write the poem or short story; stimulus points to encourage creative thinking and writing; an autobiographical piece by each writer; suggested further reading.

Each writer can be studied in isolation, but there are occasions when comparisons can contribute towards understanding and appreciation.

PART I

The Challenge
of the Blank Page

Pleasure and pain

Working with words should first and foremost be fun. Inventing
stories, playing with language and ideas, and taking advantage of
the many literary devices at your fingertips can all bring you a lot
of pleasure.

Writing is also about taking risks. You have to dare to be
vulnerable, particularly if others are going to see your work. But
only by doing this can you practise and improve. As the narrator
writes towards the end of Iain Crichton Smith's story 'The
Travelling Poet', ' . . . I shall never write again. Unless I am
willing to accept the risk of bad poems.'

Tools of the trade

If you have a favourite pen or pencil and some paper that you
actively enjoy writing on, then this can add to your pleasure in
creative writing.

However, writing is essentially about communicating. There

are many different types of communication. For example, there are facts ('The chemist is open on Sundays'), instructions ('Keep to the left!') and opinions ('I think we're in for a good summer'). Sometimes opinions are stated as if they were facts ('There are too many dogs in this country') in order to give them more authority, but it doesn't make them any more true. Use your own judgement to decide whether a fact is being stated or whether an opinion is being expressed.

Then there's description. Description is not the most effective method of communicating. If the rug has caught fire, you need to be told where the fire extinguisher is. You don't need a vivid description of its exact shade of red, or of the texture and colour of the worn, brown leather strap holding it to the wooden panel beside the radiator . . . Description is more like entertainment, self-indulgence, the icing on the communication cake. Description, in creative writing, sets up atmosphere, evokes emotion, gives background information, and can be immensely effective and rewarding when done well.

Nouns and adjectives

Nouns are naming words – hat, pigeon, shoe, window-sill. Adjectives are words which describe nouns – a *green* hat; a *crooning* pigeon; a *black*, *crêpe-soled* shoe; a *crumbling*, *mossy* window-sill/a *freshly-whitewashed* window-sill/a *sun-washed* window-sill.

Notice the difference between the three window-sills. The first two are described using factual adjectives, but the third example opens out into something more evocative, more poetic, offering the reader the idea of the sun as a cleansing, warming, optimistic force.

When you describe something, think carefully about your choice of adjective. Don't go for the easy option. Think of the most effective and appropriate word. And try not to use long strings of adjectives. One or two should be sufficient. Try to avoid too many compound or hyphenated ('crêpe-soled') adjectives – they can be cumbersome.

Concrete and abstract nouns

A concrete noun is something definite, something which exists, something your senses can confirm objectively – pen, smoke, petal, earth, sweetness, warmth.

An abstract noun is something intangible, invisible, silent, tasteless and odourless – loss, eternity, consideration, opinion, purpose, obsession.

With concrete nouns, the message is conveyed to the reader immediately: 'The dog ate my dinner.'

With abstract nouns, a smokescreen of ambiguity can develop between reader and writer: 'The result was greeted with unanimous approval.' 'Result' could refer to a race, an election or an exam. There is no concrete 'touchstone' to give the reader the full sense of the words.

Any writing that uses only concrete nouns risks superficiality. Any writing that uses only abstract nouns may become incomprehensible. In the middle lies a healthy balance.

Verbs and adverbs

Adjectives and nouns are static. Verbs, or doing words, are what make things move. 'She put on the green hat.' 'She hauled the green hat over her wayward curls.' The verbs 'put (on)' and 'hauled' give the sentences movement and life.

Adverbs are words which describe a verb. They usually end in -ly. *Quickly, endlessly, hurriedly* and *fiercely* are all adverbs. So, too, are *often, soon* and *well* (as in 'he did well').

It's easy to become lazy and overuse adverbs simply because you don't take the time to choose the best verb. If you say 'She ran down the road,' then the verb 'ran' contains the idea of speed. If you put in an adverb – 'She ran quickly down the road' – you don't really add anything. In fact, what you do is cancel out the idea of speed contained in both 'ran' and 'quickly'. The statement is weaker and sloppier than it needs to be. 'She ran very quickly down the road' would be even weaker.

But what if you want to convey the idea of speed? Think of another verb. ('She raced down the road.') Or think of a verb which compares her to a very fast animal. ('She hared down the road.') With the right verb, there is often no need for an adverb. So, if you find yourself using one, check to see if you can change the verb instead.

Simile

A simile is a figure of speech in which two things are compared using the words 'like' or 'as'. For example, if you wanted to say someone had dark hair, you could say 'She had dark hair'. If you wanted to say it in a more creative way, you could think of something to which you could compare the hair, and use a simile. 'Her hair was as black as tar.' How good a comparison is that? The hair and the tar are both black, but there the similarity ends. Can you think of a better comparison?

'Her hair was as black as a raven's wing.' The colour is right, feathers and hair are both outer coverings on living creatures, and they can both be groomed. As an object for comparison, the raven's wing is more appropriate than tar.

'Her hair was like the midnight sea on a moonless night.' This is more poetic, but the comparison could be effective in a romantic setting. Notice how the word 'dark' is suggested by the words 'midnight sea'. This simile also conveys the idea of movement, of wavy hair, and invites the reader to bring to the writing his or her own feelings about the sea on a dark night – fear, secrecy, excitement?

A simile can plant ideas in the reader's mind through the associations the comparison brings with it. Choose appropriately – the idea of comparing dark hair to tar may have to be rejected because tar is associated with stickiness and road surfaces as well as with blackness.

Metaphor

A metaphor is figure of speech in which one thing is said to **be** another:

'He was a square peg in a round hole' means that he was **like** a square peg in a round hole; that he didn't fit in.

'Her eyes were flint' means that her eyes were **like** flint; they were cold, hard and dark, yet capable of sparking.

A metaphor is one step along the way from a simile – instead of saying something is **like** something else, you may say it **is** something else. Use metaphors sparingly!

Personification

This is when personality is ascribed to something which isn't human. 'The tree sighed.' 'The brook babbled.' 'The hinges groaned.' It's a useful technique to use when you want to create atmosphere and draw the reader into the setting. You can also use it to create sympathy, fear or suspense. Daniel O'Rourke's poem 'Clockwork' (p. 67) and Helen Lamb's 'Solitude' (p. 112) provide examples of personification.

Onomatopoeia

This is tricky to spell (pronounce it on-oh-mat-oh-PAY-ah). It's a fun device to use, however, because it describes a word that sounds like its meaning. Buzz, click, hiss, thump, crash . . . Useful in adventure comics, and for evoking the sound of what you're describing.

Balancing description and narrative

If your writing is nothing but description, then the story will become static. You need to balance narrative with description to give the reader a full picture of both events and context (physical and emotional). The best writing combines both.

Narrative and chronology

Narrative is retelling a series of events in an ordered way. For example, if someone asks you to tell them what happened, your response – this, then that, then this and finally this – is a narrative.

In our daily lives we tend to be strongly chronological. One thing happens after another and that is the way we live, the way we talk about events and very often, too, the way we write about events.

However, as a creative writer, you can experiment with narrative which isn't chronological. You can use flashback, when you start at one point, then go back into the past, then come back again to the present of your story. This is structurally more complicated than simply starting at the beginning and working your way through to the end.

Most of the stories in the book do use a chronological narrative, although Janice Galloway's 'two fragments', Ian Rankin's 'Scarab' and Iain Crichton Smith's 'The Travelling Poet' do not.

Poetry and narrative

Some poems are strongly narrative, like 'The Ancient Mariner' by Samuel Taylor Coleridge or 'The Owl and the Pussycat' by Edward Lear, where stories are told in verse. However, much modern poetry is not essentially narrative.

Many of the poems in this book are not primarily retelling a series of events. Instead they are non-narrative. They are exploring ideas and thoughts rather than detailing one happening after another. The intention of the poet is not to tell you about something, but to make you react intellectually or emotionally;

to give you insight into the way they think or feel about something. Poetry is often concerned more with thoughts and emotions, rather than events. If you compare 'Little Blue Blue' by Edwin Morgan (p. 32) with 'In The Skip' by Brian McCabe (p. 49) you will find that the former is narrative to a degree, where the latter is presenting observations and ideas, rather than dealing with events.

It is impossible to draw hard lines between narrative and non-narrative writing. You can use both poetry and prose to retell events or deal with ideas. It is more common, though, to find narrative in prose, and ideas in poetry.

Inspiration and 'Gifts'

Finding ideas to write about can be very difficult and frustrating. However, you should be able to draw comfort from Part 2 of this book, in which many of the writers describe their sources of inspiration.

Often, ideas come from real life – from something that has happened to the writer or to someone else. Often, too, real events have to be altered for the good of the story or poem. This is because reality can be too disorganised or too coincidental – it may have happened in real life, but this won't make it plausible in a story. But reality as a springboard into creative writing is very valuable. Both Iain Crichton Smith (p. 95) and Moira Burgess (p. 129) draw the distinction between the 'I' voice they use in their stories and their true selves. They have both separated themselves from the text and invented a persona. This gives them the freedom to be, on the page, someone who thinks and speaks and behaves in a different way, yet they can still write with the immediacy of the first person narrative.

Several of the writers mention the idea of a 'gift' catalyst which has inspired their work. For Iain Crichton Smith it was a visitor, for Gordon Meade it was the idea of circus performers, for Edwin Morgan it was a misprint, for Valerie Gillies it was four taps on the soundboard of a harp. Such gifts are there for you, too. However, if you're not attuned to picking them up, they will pass you by. Try to open your mind to heightened moments like these, where the unexpected suddenly connects and sparks off an idea.

You can also discover 'gifts' when you're writing. If you're unsure about a phrase or an image you've used, stop and listen to your inner voice. You can be certain that if you've noticed something not quite right, not quite as good as it could be, a reader will be affected by it, too. They may not consciously analyse the weakness, but your writing won't be working as effectively as it should. So, start crafting. Change the image or the idea. Dare to take chances with changes and you may well get lucky and find more than you were looking for – gifts.

Redrafting is also a valuable part of the critical appraisal process. When you are working out how the writers in this book have achieved certain effects, try removing their words and replacing them with others. What effect does this have? Why is the author's version better?

Subject and theme

If you are unsure about concrete and abstract nouns, read the section on p. 5 again before going any further.

There are two levels of response when it comes to working out what a piece of writing is about.

The first level is expressed in concrete, factual terms. It's the straightforward, simple answer to the question: what is the poem or story about?

For example, let's take the story of Julie who sets off to buy a parrot. On the way to the pet shop, she sees a sign – 'Urgent! Six Adorable Kittens Free to Good Homes' – and comes back with a kitten instead.

On the most obvious and immediate level, this is a story about Julie who goes to buy one pet and comes back with another.

That is a factual statement using concrete nouns. It's the subject of the story. It tells us nothing about Julie's thoughts or feelings or motivation.

The second level, or 'the theme', is more complex and more abstract. It concerns the idea *behind* the story. Without reading the whole story in our example, it's difficult to know what the theme is, but it could be loneliness (Julie needs a pet in her life), the exploitation of exotic creatures (Julie may feel uneasy about keeping a parrot confined in a cage), poverty (parrots are expensive) or changing values (Julie may have wanted the parrot as a status symbol, but realised the shallowness of that when faced with homeless kittens).

All of these thematic ideas are expressed in abstract terms – loneliness, exploitation, poverty and changing values.

In every piece of creative writing, you will find that there is a straightforward, simple subject – what the story is about in the most concrete terms – and a theme (or set of themes), which is the idea or concept the story explores.

When you are writing, you can start from either end. For example, you can decide you want to write on the theme of bullying, and then think of a specific situation to illustrate it. Or you can decide to write about a child who runs away from school. You might then find yourself dealing with themes such as bullying, fear and isolation.

Be aware of these two levels in your creative writing.

Think about other kinds of writing – recipes, technical manuals, biography, newspaper and magazine articles. To what extent do the two levels apply to each of these?

Syntax, vocabulary and the vernacular

Syntax is sentence structure, or the way you choose to order words. For example, the following statement about unsweetened coffee can be rephrased, using exactly the same words, in a number of different ways.

Given the choice, I prefer not to have sugar in my coffee.
Given the choice, I prefer to not have sugar in my coffee.
I prefer not to have sugar in my coffee, given the choice.
I prefer, given the choice, not to have sugar in my coffee.

Each of these four sentences has a slightly different effect and emphasis: the syntax of each is different.

Your vocabulary is the word bank you have in your head from which you select when you write or speak. We all have different vocabularies, although there's enough overlap for us to be able to communicate with any other English speaker. However, English is such a rich language that there are often many different ways of saying the same thing and each will have its own particular impact.

I'd like some of your lemonade.
Give me a drink of your lemonade.
That lemonade'll go down a treat.
Gie's a slug o' yer ginger.

The first two examples are formal requests, the third is less formal. The fourth, which has the same syntax as the second, illustrates not only different vocabulary, but also the vernacular. In this case, Glaswegian, where 'us' (as in 'gie's' = 'give us') is used in place of 'me'. 'Slug' is Standard English for a single gulp, although it is not commonly used, but 'ginger' is vernacular, or Glaswegian dialect, for all soft drinks.

Syntax, vocabulary and the vernacular (or dialect) are complex, interconnecting concepts. You will be aware of their effect, but possibly only subconsciously. By becoming consciously aware of them, you can exploit their potential for effect.

A particular style of syntax will often be linked to a particular vocabulary. For example, where one person might say 'I've just finished a jam sandwich' another might say 'I'm just after having a piece and jam'. If you look at the stories in this book by Janice Galloway (p. 79) and Alison Kermack (p. 118), you will find examples of the vernacular with its own idiosyncratic syntax. All the writers in this book use their own particular syntax and vocabulary, although some styles are more obviously distinctive than others.

You, too, will have your own syntax and vocabulary, as you have your own speech patterns and verbal mannerisms. If you become aware of them, then you have the power to change them if you wish. This is similar to the separation process mentioned on p. 9, where 'you' and 'your writing' become two distinct entities.

Characterisation and dialogue

Characterisation means creating characters. This involves two separate processes. First, you get to know your character(s) and, secondly, you select information to communicate to your reader.

It helps if you have a good picture of a character in your head before you begin writing. You may not use all the details you have decided on, but your character will be more rounded if you have given him or her careful consideration.

Unusual details can be most evocative, so use your senses. What do your characters look like? What do they wear? How do they wear it? What kind of sounds do they make – can you describe their voices, their footsteps, their verbal mannerisms? How do they smell – pleasant, unpleasant, natural or artificial? Taste and touch can also be used in characterisation, although these are more intimate traits.

Remember, names come with associations. They may suggest the character is old-fashioned, exotic, aristocratic, babied or despised. You can choose names which are affectionate diminutives or associated with screen or pop stars. But whatever names you choose, think about the associations first.

There are other components that make your characters individuals: their work, recreation, attitudes and beliefs.

Characters will be more effective if they are shown to be doing something at a specific time and place in your story. Your characters should also change or develop during the narrative –

only cardboard cutouts are untouched by the course of events.

Don't forget the past. What has happened to make your characters the way they are? How do they feel about themselves? How do they interact with others? What is the driving force in their lives?

If you've been thorough in your characterisation, then you will know exactly how your character speaks, which brings us to direct speech and those individual speech patterns which were mentioned earlier.

Direct speech is when you put the actual words spoken by your character into the text. It is also a powerful characterising device. For example, you can say that Jack asked for an apple. This is indirect or reported speech, because we do not know the exact words that Jack said. It is a far weaker way of writing than if you use direct speech. Jack can ask for an apple in many different ways; each time he is a different person.

'Gimme that apple there!'
'Please may I have an apple?'
'No, not that one! The Granny Smith!'
'Pleez, give me apple?'

Don't shy away from characterising using direct speech. Most of the stories here and some of the poems use direct speech. Try to imagine how drab they would be if everything were in indirect speech.

Conflict and change

The importance of both conflict and change in creative writing cannot be overestimated. If you think about the opposites – harmony and stability – and consider using one or the other as a springboard for a piece of writing, it soon becomes obvious that it will be a struggle to get anywhere if nothing changes and everyone's happy.

Conflict is the more dramatic of the two driving forces. If Mrs Sharp, in Agnes Owens's story 'Getting Sent For' (p. 39), agreed with and co-operated fully with the headmistress, there would have been no story. If John's exam had been easy in Bernard MacLaverty's 'The Miraculous Candidate' (p. 55), then again there would have been no story.

The conflict doesn't have to be between two people; it can be any kind of conflicting tension which drives the narrative. It can also be a character in conflict with him or herself. But a problem, a disagreement, hostility – conflict in the widest sense – is essential as a guiding force in a piece of writing.

Change is a milder driving force than conflict. It is subtler but equally effective. Change is behind Alison Kermack's 'A Wee Tatty' (p. 118) and Ian Rankin's 'Scarab' (p. 150). It is also the impetus behind many of the poems featured in this book: 'The Old Woman's Reel' (p. 73), 'Hollow' (p. 106), 'The Sedated' (p. 124) and 'The Apple Ghost' (p. 143).

Look for change or conflict as a driving force behind your writing. There's nothing worse than trying to write about someone who is perfectly happy doing nothing.

Prose logic and poetic logic

We are now going to consider the difference between a short story and a poem. Why should a piece of writing become one or the other? Are they two separate distinct art forms, or is there an overlap?

Prose logic is the logic of common sense. If the sweet pea petals have all been blown away, it's because the wind's too strong. If you are locked out, it's because you've forgotten your key, or because the locks have been changed.

Poetic logic is the logic of emotional sense, of fantasy, of lateral as opposed to linear thinking. It's a logic of magic or nonsense, and yet there's a truth, a poetic truth, in it.

For example, the sweet pea petals that are missing – a poetically logical solution could have them taking flight with the butterflies that visit them, becoming winged creatures in their own right. And if you're locked out, then the look or the apology or the outstretched hand may well be the key to the door of isolation.

This is an important distinction to be aware of. Look at the following poems: 'In the Skip' (p. 49), 'Joy' (p. 88), 'Solitude' (p. 112), 'The Sedated' (p. 124), 'Second Infancy' (p. 138) and 'The Apple Ghost' (p. 144). You will find poetic logic at work in all of them.

In most of the short stories in this book you will find prose logic. One story, however, does cross over into poetic logic – 'The Travelling Poet' (p. 95). The writer, Iain Crichton Smith, is also a poet.

You can also find examples of prose logic working in some of the poems – 'Little Blue Blue' (p. 32), combines both logics, and there are elements of prose logic in the poems 'Compare and Contrast' (p. 27), 'Hollow' (p. 106) and 'The Scottish National Cushion Survey' (p. 162).

Thus the boundaries between prose and poetry are perhaps not as clearly defined as we might like to think. The next section, on plot and endings, explores this idea further.

Plot and endings

The plot is the series of events or revelations that unfolds as your writing progresses from the beginning to the end. You can think of a plot as a series of obstacles which your main character has to overcome in order to achieve what he or she wants. This is where conflict and change can be involved.

For example, let's start with our hero, Davy, who wants to become the best highboard diver in the world. He can train hard and win gold and we don't have a story. On the other hand, he might have enormous difficulty finding someone to coach him, finding a pool to train in, raising the money, making the time, losing his friends, falling behind with his schoolwork – all problems he has to overcome to achieve his goal; all possible plot devices for a writer to explore. Now this kind of long timescale might be better suited to a novel, but it can also be the background to a short story where you select the most dramatic point, the turning point, in Davy's diving career.

Perhaps it is the big day, his one chance to prove himself. Something goes wrong. Someone he cares for more than his diving suddenly needs him. Perhaps his mother has an accident. He doesn't know what to do. He may pull out to be with her. She might not want him to. He may go ahead anyway and dive, for her. He may win, he may mess it up completely, she might die, he might finally realise that people matter more than diving, or that for him, diving matters more than people. But whatever happens, you have to have some kind of a plot, some kind of progression and development.

You may not know the ending of your story when you first start to write it, or, alternatively, you may be unable to begin unless you *do* know the ending, but, either way, the text will need to be tightened up and edited and redrafted as you go along. (None of the stories in this book happened by chance. They were all crafted from initial idea to final draft.) You will often find that the seed for a story's ending is planted right at the beginning, often so skilfully that you don't notice first time around. This is something you, too, can do.

Endings are crucial. Not because your stories must stop some time, but because they must stop at the right point and in the right way. The best endings are unexpected and yet inevitable. They should leave the reader feeling satisfied and without unanswered questions, unless, as with 'Scarab' (p. 150), this is the author's intention.

A twist ending can be particularly effective, although not all stories are suited to this device. Such endings involve a turnaround in events – information is revealed which was previously unknown to the reader, and everything that has come before suddenly shifts into a different perspective. Of the seven stories in this book, only 'two fragments' (p. 79) and 'The Travelling Poet' (p. 95) do not feature twist endings. The authors of these stories are aiming for something other than the thrill factor of surprising the reader. Look at both these stories and see what effect Janice Galloway and Iain Crichton Smith manage to create with their endings.

As with all other aspects of your writing, you have choices. Knowing what they are simply extends your range and no particular form of ending is better or worse than any other.

Poems, too, need endings. Nowadays, many poems do not follow a narrative structure. That is, they do not tell stories. But they, too, don't just stop. As with a story, the best ending to a poem is unexpected and yet inevitable. Twist endings are also quite common, but these are founded on a poetic rather than a prose logic. Look, for example, at 'In the Skip' (p. 49), 'Clockwork' (p. 67), 'The Old Woman's Reel' (p. 73) for evidence of poetically twisted endings. A good ending is often difficult to engineer, but if you keep a wide open mind and make lots of notes, then you might be lucky and some magic, some gift, will fall into place for you and you'll wonder why you didn't think of it before.

Poetry, rhythm and rhyme

Some people prefer to write poetry, others prefer prose and there are others still who write both, finding each satisfies a different aspect of their creativity. It should be clear by now that the boundaries between poetry and prose are not as clearly defined as you might at first think.

So what *does* separate poetry from prose? Many of the literary devices useful in prose are also used in poetry, but there are one or two additional tools exclusive to poetry.

You can tell at a glance if a piece of writing is prose or poetry because of its shape on the page, its form. Poetry is written in lines and verses, instead of paragraphs. Line breaks become weighted with significance because they produce a visual pause, a kind of punctuation, which gives each line its own weight. The following line can then modify the meaning of the previous one. You can find clear examples of this in Gordon Meade's poem 'The Sedated' (p. 124) and Elissa Soave's 'Hollow' (p. 106).

There is rhythm and rhyme in both prose and poetry. For example, in 'two fragments' (p. 79) Janice Galloway likens amputated fingers to 'the stumpy tops of two pink pork links'. The phrase has a chopped-up rhythm, and the rhyme and alliteration make it comically gruesome. (Alliteration is the repetition of the same sound for literary effect. Here, Janice Galloway uses alliteration on the sharp plosive consonants 't', 'p' and 'k' for impact. The phrase 'fancy phosphorescence' is also alliterative on both 'f' and 's' sounds, though they are spelled in different ways.)

However, both rhythms and rhyme are often more noticeable, more finely tuned, in poetry. The rhythm can be regular, as in a nursery rhyme, where you can tap your foot to it, or subtle, allowing the graceful cadence or sharp shock of a phrase to affect you on a subliminal level. Rhyme, too, can be insistent, again as in a nursery rhyme, or it can be concealed yet still effective in half-rhymes, assonance and internal rhyming.

Half-rhymes are when the consonant sound remains the same, but the vowel sound is different. For example, when Valerie Gillies rhymes 'her / there' or 'window / now' in her poem 'The Old Woman's Reel' (p. 73), it isn't because she can't think of a full rhyme, but because she wants the subtler effect of the half-rhyme.

Assonance is the counterpart of half-rhyme, when the vowel sounds remain the same but the consonants change. For example, when Edwin Morgan writes 'five feet / high' or 'messages without measure' in his poem 'Little Blue Blue' (p. 32) he is using assonance first on the long 'i' sound, then on the short 'e' sound. Also, you will find assonance in the last verse of John Glenday's poem, 'The Apple Ghost' (p. 144) on the 'oo' sound.

Normally, rhymes are found at the end of the line. Internal rhyming is where rhyming is within the lines. For an example, let's look at the first three lines of Edwin Morgan's poem, 'Little Blue Blue':

The mirror caught him as he straightened his sky-blue tie,
he was the son of sky and sea, five
feet high with wings furled, flexing . . .

There are four pure rhymes – 'sky / tie / sky / high' – and only one of them is at the end of the line. This is internal rhyming. (In addition, Edwin Morgan uses assonance with the word 'five'.)

One technique which is used more in poetry than in prose is poetic compression. Poems have to be read more slowly than prose because of this compression of language. They are seldom read only once and they often repay study, when the rich layers of meaning that result from poetic compression can be discovered. This topic is dealt with more fully in the 'Creative writing and thinking' section following John Glenday's poem, 'The Apple Ghost' (p. 144). If this kind of compression is used constantly in prose, then it can become thick, cloying and difficult to read. However, as Iain Crichton Smith demonstrates, used judiciously it is most effective.

Rhythm is a complicated issue and the following section on 'Pace' includes further discussion of rhythm.

Pace

Pace, in writing, is about the speed, both slow and fast, with which a writer conveys information. It is affected by both vocabulary and sentence length and how much detail the writer goes into. Generally the shorter the sentences or phrases, and the shorter the words, the faster the pace. For example, we could write:

> Marie entered her car and inserted the keys into the ignition. She started the engine, took off the handbrake, let in the clutch and pressed her right foot down hard on the accelerator pedal. The car moved off very quickly and the tyres screeched behind her.

There's something wrong, isn't there? The pace is wrong. It's not fast enough. There's too much irrelevant detail and too many big words.

Marie took the wheel, fired the engine and put her foot down. The car screeched off.

Better? Shall we slow it down?

Marie sat in the car. She was surrounded by maps and guide books. She glanced at the clock; it flickered 2.47 and she yawned. In her hand she could feel the cool metal of the ignition key, and the absurdity of the woollen pom-pom which her daughter had tied on to the key-ring. She wondered whether she should start the engine yet, or wait a little bit longer.

This is different again, isn't it? This is slow, with long sentences and very little happening. It is reflective, moody and with a little suspense – why is Marie waiting?

You, too, can deliberately pace your writing, by being aware of the effect of content and detail, sentence length and word length.

These are examples of pace in prose, but often the effect is more noticeable in poetry, where rhythm is exploited to either drive the poem along, or slow it down. If you look at 'Little Blue Blue' by Edwin Morgan (p. 32), you will find him using pace and rhythm in two different ways. The difference is highlighted by the layout on the page. Try saying the first verse and snapping your fingers in time to the rhythm. It's not very accommodating. In other words, it's not in regular rhythm. Try snapping your fingers to the second, short, indented verse and it works a treat. This is both rhythm and pace in action.

If you're still uncertain about prose rhythms and poetic rhythms, you can try this exercise. Instead of using the right words, make only the sound 'daa' in place of the words. (Yes, it sounds silly!) Now say the nursery rhyme 'Hickory Dickory Dock' to yourself and hear the rhythm isolated in 'daa's. Then, re-read this paragraph in 'daa's and you'll soon appreciate the lack of regularity in normal prose rhythms.

Symbolism

Symbolism is found in both poetry and prose. If an object becomes a symbol, then it represents something in addition to what it actually is. For example, a book is something you read, but a book can also be seen as a symbol of learning. Green is a colour, but it can symbolise inexperience, ecological awareness or envy. When something becomes a symbol, it represents an abstract concept. Symbolism is another way of getting to grips with intangibles.

This subject is dealt with further in the section following Ian Rankin's story, 'Scarab' (p. 150).

Irony and black humour

Irony is when words or a situation subsequently backfire on someone. That sounds complicated, but an example will make it clear. Let's say Graham is going to hang a picture on the wall. All he needs to do is hammer in a nail. 'It won't take a minute: it's easy!' he says, but then he hits his thumb with the hammer and has to go to Casualty for stitches. Blood from his thumb has stained the carpet, so he has to have that cleaned. When he finally recovers enough to drive the nail into the wall, the wall crumbles and he has to replaster and redecorate.

That's an exaggerated example, but it makes Graham's remark about the speed and ease of the task heavily ironic. There's a famous-last-words element to verbal irony.

An ironic situation is where fate conspires against someone and makes his or her actions futile. For example, if Graham, having been through all that bother to hammer a nail into the wall, then discovers the picture doesn't match the room, or is the wrong size, or the nail is in the wrong place, then the situation becomes ironic.

Irony and black humour are closely related. Black humour is when something essentially tragic is related in such a way that we end up laughing. We may be shocked at ourselves for laughing, and be accused of having a sick sense of humour, but it is a psychological escape valve for the unbearable events in life.

An example of black humour? A couple and their pet dog are on holiday abroad. They don't speak the language. They're hungry and go into a restaurant. They point at the dog, then at their mouths, indicating, they think, that they'd like their dog to be fed. The dog is led away. When they finish their delicious meal, and ask for their dog to be returned, they discover they've eaten it.

Janice Galloway's story, 'two fragments' (p. 79), Alison Kermack's story, 'A Wee Tatty' (p. 118) and Moira Burgess's story, 'Surrogate' (p. 129), exploit irony and black humour.

Plagiarism and learning to write

Plagiarism is a deliberate and deceitful act of literary theft. It involves someone stealing another writer's words and passing them off as his or her own.

If you find a phrase you like in one of the pieces in this book and you lift it and slip it into a piece of your own, that is plagiarism. If you copy out one of the stories and change a word here and a phrase or two there, and perhaps change the location and the names, that, too, is plagiarism.

However, writers have to learn to write. And writers study other writers. As Bernard MacLaverty says, he copied other authors' *ways* of writing, citing Kafka, Joyce and Gerard Manley Hopkins. The crucial distinction is that he was studying how they used language, the kinds of themes and subjects they dealt with, the way they structured their writing.

In this book you are often asked to analyse the way a writer is working words. Then you are asked to write something yourself which gives you practice in applying the skills you have observed. You are told to steer well clear of whatever particular area the writer has been dealing with and the results will be all your own work. This is not plagiarism. This is learning to write and, as

Bernard MacLaverty went on to discover, this will lead you to find your own voice, your own style and your own strengths.

Time

Time is essential for writing.

Obviously, you need time to put words down on paper.

You also need time to think. As Alison Kermack says, this is not sitting down and thinking, this is something that your mind is doing most of the time, whatever the rest of you is doing. It's free-wheeling mentally, when your thoughts go wherever. Ideas flit in and out, and are stored, developed or rejected.

When you do get an idea, you need time to write it down. Alison Kermack found inspiration just when she was about to settle down for the night. This is a good time, and maybe the only time your subconscious mind can become conscious. But if you can't at least make a note of the idea there and then, it'll be gone by morning.

Sometimes a lot of time has to elapse before a piece of writing becomes possible. Maybe years. You can store incidents and memories for no good reason and then, one day, something will click and it will all fall into place. Many of the writers in this book describe how inspiration came as a result of ancient memories connecting with other recent or even current events.

When you've written a piece, you also need time to distance yourself from it. You can be far too close to your writing to be able to see it with any objectivity. Yet you need objectivity to be able to appraise your own work. You have to put it aside for long enough so that when you come back to it, days or weeks later, you feel as if a different 'you' had written it.

Titles

These usually materialise after you've finished writing your poem or story. There's not really much to say about them, other than that they should be appropriate. If they can add something to the writing, then all well and good. Many titles are simply labels, others may be cryptic (only making sense when the reader gets to the end), and others may be punning and amusing. You should take some time – again! – over your titles and make sure they fit your work.

Useful reference books

There are a couple of reference books which can be of use to a writer. That may sound cautiously worded and it is, because dependency on, or overuse of reference books can shackle your creativity.

The first book is a good dictionary. *Chambers 20th Century Dictionary* is one of several good ones. It is especially interesting as it contains many Scots words missing from English dictionaries. As the official Scrabble dictionary, it also features many weird and wonderful words that are worth lots of points on the right squares! Seriously, though, if you're working with words you need to know that they do mean *exactly* what you think they might. They may have other meanings that you don't want to imply. Also, if you're studying other writers' work, they may have used words with hidden depths which a good dictionary can reveal to you.

For example, take the word 'carnation' – this is a pretty flower, with an exotic clove scent, associated with celebrations and ceremonies. But if you look it up in a good dictionary, an etymological one which gives the derivation of the word, you'll find it comes from the Latin word for flesh. That cluster of raw, red serrated petals will blossom into connotations of wounding and pain. A rose, on the other hand, as the dictionary can confirm, comes without such complex associations. Dictionaries are fun to read and you can learn a lot from them.

The second reference book to keep to hand is *Roget's Thesaurus*. This is essentially a series of lists of synonyms. It's interesting to browse through and it can be very valuable if you're writing a poem and want to avoid repetition. Used in conjunction with a dictionary, it may help you to find 'gifts'. However, watch that you don't start using big words just to show off your new-found vocabulary. Your first concern must always be your piece of writing and if a flashy word is going to be dazzlingly out of place, then think again.

Finally

Working words into poems or stories should be a pleasure. Many of the writers in this book talk of hard work, but the overall impression is surely the satisfaction of producing a piece of writing you can be proud of. Good luck.

PART 2

Words in Action

COMPARE AND CONTRAST
Norman MacCaig

The great thinker died
after forty years of poking about
with his little torch
in the dark forest of ideas,
in the bright glare of perception,
leaving a legacy of fourteen books
to the world
where a hen disappeared
into six acres of tall oats
and sauntered unerringly
to the nest with five eggs in it.

Questions and thinking points

1 Explain why there should be no questions on this poem!

2 When you think about the theme of the poem, in what way
   does the writing of it become ironic?

Now read what Norman MacCaig writes about 'Compare and Contrast':

 I've often thought of the extraordinary things animals do, like the hen in 'Compare and Contrast'. The 'great thinker' in the poem could no more have found the nest than he could have laid the eggs in it. Or think of the migratory birds who fly from South Africa to Scotland, to the same square yard they were born in, etc,. etc., etc.

(I know that hen and saw it return to its nest – no bother.)

And yet we're so proud of our brains. *Homo sapiens*, indeed. Just think of how they're behaving in most of our countries in the world. I don't like Mankind, though I like Johnny and Jeannie and Mary and Malcolm and plenty more.

3 In this poem, Norman MacCaig finds the innate skills of birds and animals far superior to the arrogance of man. Why is the choice of a hen particularly effective? Think beyond 'because it's true'; what if it had been a very different kind of animal? How would the poem have been affected?

4 In what ways are the 'great thinker' and the hen similar? And different?

5 What good and bad is there in comparing and contrasting?

Creative thinking and writing

To a certain extent, Norman MacCaig is playing devil's advocate here, writing tongue-in-cheek with a wry, dry sense of humour. This can be a good stance to adopt if you are trying to get an angle on a piece of writing. This can prompt conflict, which is often a catalyst for creativity.

But, first and foremost, the poem is crafted. Look at the

vocabulary, the structure, the use of numbers, the wrapping up of the message in images, the concrete illustration of an abstract concept.

■ *See if you can think of a provocative stance to take on something commonly acknowledged as 'inferior'. For example, a hen is not normally rated above a great philosopher. Take perhaps another animal or insect, normally considered lowly, and think about a way, or ways, in which it can be superior to humans. Decide the subject, find the images and craft the piece into a poem.*

On himself and his writing

Norman MacCaig

I started to write, I think, when at school, aged 16, the English teacher told us to write either an essay or a poem. The poem was shorter. I discovered I liked writing verses, and have written them ever since.

I was born and have lived most of my life in Edinburgh, but the north-west Highlands and the Hebrides have always been very important to me. Much of my writing is about those areas.

I earned my living as a teacher in schools and universities, which I also enjoyed.

Further reading

You'll find more poems by Norman MacCaig in the following selected books, all published by Chatto & Windus:

Collected Poems
A World of Difference
The Equal Skies
Voice Over

If you are interested in the idea of animals being superior to humans, you might enjoy the short stories of Hector Hugh Munro, who wrote under the name of Saki. He was writing around the time of the First World War and collections of his stories are available from libraries and bookshops.

LITTLE BLUE BLUE

Edwin Morgan

(misprinted title of Norman MacCaig's 'Little Boy Blue' in *The Equal Skies*, 1980)

The mirror caught him as he straightened his sky-blue tie,
he was the son of sky and sea, five
feet high with wings furled, flexing
and shifting the sheen of his midnight blue
mohair tuxedo, tightening his saxe plastic belt
one notch, slicing the room with Gillette-blue eyes,
padding to the door in dove-blue brushed suede boots,
pinning his buttonhole periwinkle with a blue shark's grin.

      Once in the street
      he got the beat
      unfurled his wing
      began to sing
      'She is, he is, she is my star'
      to his electric blue guitar.

Little Blue Blue flew to the land of denim,
bought himself jeans and a denim jacket and a denim cap,
what blue, what blue, he cried, and tried his jeans
with his mohair dinner-jacket, tried his mohair trousers
with his denim bomber jacket, tried his denim cap
with his saxe-blue belt and his dove-blue boots and a
navy-blue Adidas bag and nothing else
till the slate-blue pigeons all blushed purple, but

      once in the street
      he got the beat
      unfurled his wing
      began to sing

'He is, she is, he is my star'
to his electric blue guitar.

Then he went to sea and sailed the blue main
in his navy jersey with his wings well battened down,
knocked up a tattoo parlour in old Yokohama,
got bluebirds on his hands and a blue pierced heart,
and a geisha-girl on his shoulder with a blue rose,
and a trail of blue hounds chasing a blue fox
into covert – oh, he said, I'm black and blue all over,
but he staggered out into that Nippon moon, and

    once in the street
    he got the beat
    unfurled his wing
    began to sing
    'She is, he is, she is my star'
    to his electric blue guitar.

Back home, he bought a cobalt Talbot Sunbeam
with aquamarine upholstery and citizens band radio,
said Blue Blue here, do you read me, do you read me?
as he whizzed up to Scrabster in his royal-blue pinstripes.
And his dashboard sent him messages without measure,
for everybody loves a blue angel, whistling
at the wheel under azure highland skies.
And he stopped at each village, and smiled like the sun, for

    once in the street
    he got the beat
    unfurled his wing
    began to sing
    'He is, she is, he is my star'
    to his electric blue guitar.

Questions and thinking points

1 Have you read this poem aloud yet? Do so!

2 Why is 'Little Blue Blue' so much fun to read aloud? (Consider rhythm, rhyme, alliteration, assonance, pace and content.)

3 How would you define the character of Little Blue Blue? List as many facets as you can, justifying your choice with reference to the poem.

4 Explain the pun in the phrase 'electric blue guitar'. How does word order contribute to this? And how does word order affect the rhythm of the phrase? Try swapping 'electric' and 'blue'. Which way sounds better and why? (See the section on 'Poetry, rhythm and rhyme' (p. 18) if you're unsure.)

Here is Norman MacCaig's poem, 'Little Boy Blue':

LITTLE BOY BLUE

Are you dreaming of the big city,
of movies and bus stops and supermarkets?
Or of some girl in swirly petticoats
crossing another field with a milking pail in her hand?

Or have you been listening to the news
on the telly? – are you taking
industrial action?

Whatever way, blow your horn for me.
For my sheep are in the meadow, my cows
are trampling the brave corn flat –
and I watch them with indifference.

You look from under your feathery hat
at me dozing under a haystack
and slowly, deliciously
close your nursery eyes that rhyme with mine.

Now read what Edwin Morgan says about 'Little Blue Blue':

❝ Anything can start off a poem – an experience, a feeling, an idea, an event, or in this case something as accidental and insignificant as a misprint. But whatever it is, it must set going a chain of verbal reactions which will eventually show the reader or listener that the poet was interested, involved, surprised, pleased, moved, or in some way galvanised by the initial happening. The writer cannot always pinpoint what that stimulus was, but in the present instance it is clear. As soon as I read 'Little Blue Blue' as the misprinted title of Norman MacCaig's poem 'Little Boy Blue' in his 1980 collection, *The Equal Skies*, I thought to myself, Aha, here is an imaginary character I can begin to see and would like to develop. Unlike the boy in the nursery rhyme who blows his horn, he would have an electric guitar, and it will be an electric blue electric guitar because everything about the boy is blue; indeed, he is a blue angel (echoes somewhere of the old Marlene Dietrich film!), and because he is an angel he sings his love-refrain addressed indifferently to both sexes. I brought in as many different kinds of blue as I could, and made him a character in a fantastic story where he travels as far as Japan but ends back in Scotland. The poem is strongly rhythmical, and could perhaps be seen as a sort of adult nursery rhyme. It asks to be spoken aloud. I wanted the image of the boy to be on one level humorous and absurd, yet at the same time something very positive, since the last we see of him is that he smiles like the sun, and everybody – don't they? – loves a blue angel. So much so, that the audience at a reading may be asked to join in the refrain. ❞

Creative thinking and writing

'Little Blue Blue' shows a creative mind playing with words. Other readers of the misprinted title might either not have noticed it, or dismissed it as only a misprint. Edwin Morgan pounced on it and ran off in glee, whirling and twirling it into a fantastic blue creation.

There are similar 'gifts' waiting everywhere for you, if you allow your mind to be receptive. Not only to misprints, but to anything – any unusual juxtaposition or fragmented remark or moment of behaviour. You can dismiss such 'gifts', or fail even to notice them, but they are there, and if you allow your mind a moment of reflection, you, too, could be running off with an idea, an image.

■ *Use Edwin Morgan's poem as the catalyst for a piece of writing of your own. (Choose another colour and another adjective.) You might find your writing 'wants' to be a poem, but it might equally turn into a short piece of prose.*

On himself and his writing

Edwin Morgan

‘ I began writing poetry at school when I was about twelve or thirteen, and have continued to do so, apart from a gap when I was in the army during the Second World War (1940–1946), ever since. I think it is an urge, rather than something you choose to do, and for that reason it is hard to explain, though I am sure the explanation must include the fact that you enjoy poetry and believe in its value. The old belief that 'a poet's born, not made' has some truth in it, if not the whole truth – since the craft of writing has to be learned, often quite gradually and painfully. Something, whether it's a vivid imagination or a love of words or more likely a mixture of both, predisposes you to try your hand at poetry, and you find yourself setting out on a long journey you could never have planned. ’

Further reading

You'll find more poems by Edwin Morgan in the following selected books:

Selected Poems (Carcanet Press)
Collected Poems (Carcanet Press)
Sonnets From Scotland (Mariscat Press)
Sweeping Out The Dark (Carcanet Press)

GETTING SENT FOR
Agnes Owens

Mrs Sharp knocked timidly on the door marked 'Headmistress'.

'Come in,' a cool voice commanded.

She shuffled in, slightly hunched, clutching a black plastic shopping bag and stood waiting for the headmistress to raise her eyes from the notebook she was engrossed in.

'Do sit down,' said the headmistress when Mrs Sharp coughed apologetically.

Mrs Sharp collapsed into a chair and placed her bag between her feet. The headmistress relinquished the notebook with a sigh and began.

'I'm sorry to bring you here, but recently George has become quite uncontrollable in class. Something will have to be done.'

Mrs Sharp shifted about in the chair and assumed a placating smile.

'Oh dear – I thought he was doing fine. I didn't know – '

'It's been six months since I spoke to you,' interrupted the headmistress, 'and I'm sorry to say he has not improved one bit. In fact he's getting steadily worse.'

Mrs Sharp met the impact of the gold-framed spectacles nervously as she said, 'It's not as if he gets away with anything at home. His Da and me are always on at him, but he pays no attention.'

The headmistress's mouth tightened. 'He will just have to pay attention.'

'What's he done this time?' Mrs Sharp asked with a surly edge to her voice.

'He runs in and out of class when the teacher's back is turned and distracts the other children.'

Mrs Sharp eased out her breath. 'Is that all?'

The headmistress was incredulous. 'Is that all? With twenty-five pupils in a class, one disruptive element can ruin everything. It's difficult enough to push things into their heads as it is – ' She broke off.

'Seems to me they're easily distracted,' said Mrs Sharp.

'Well children are, you know.' The headmistress allowed a frosty smile to crease her lips.

'Maybe he's not the only one who runs about,' observed Mrs Sharp mildly.

'Mrs Sharp, I assure you George is the main troublemaker, otherwise I would not have sent for you.'

The light from the headmistress's spectacles was as blinding as a torch.

Mrs Sharp shrank back. 'I'm not meaning to be cheeky, but George isn't a bad boy. I can hardly credit he's the worst in the class.'

The headmistress conceded. 'No, I wouldn't say he's the worst. There are some pupils I've washed my hands of. As yet there's still hope for George. That's why I sent for you. If he puts his mind to it he can work quite well, but let's face it, if he's going to continue the way he's doing, he'll end up in a harsher place than this school.'

Mrs Sharp beamed as if she was hearing fulsome praise. 'You mean he's clever?'

'I wouldn't say he's clever,' said the headmistress cautiously, 'but he's got potential. But really,' she snapped, 'it's more his behaviour than his potential that worries us.'

Mrs Sharp tugged her wispy hair dreamily. 'I always knew George had it in him. He was such a bright baby. Do you know he opened his eyes and stared straight at me when he was a day old. Sharp by name, and sharp by nature – that's what his Da always said.'

'That may be,' said the headmistress, taking off her spectacles and rubbing her eyes, 'but sharp is not what I'm looking for.'

Then, aware of Mrs Sharp's intent inspection of her naked face, she quickly replaced them, adding, 'Another thing. He never does his homework.'

'I never knew he got any,' said Mrs Sharp, surprised. 'Mind you we've often asked him "Don't you get any homework?" and straight away he answers "We don't get any" – '

The headmistress broke in. 'He's an incorrigible liar.'

'Liar?' Mrs Sharp clutched the collar of her bottle-green coat.

'Last week he was late for school. He said it was because you made him stay and tidy his room.'

Mrs Sharp's eyes flickered. 'What day was that?'

'Last Tuesday.' The headmistress leaned over her desk. 'Did you?'

'I don't know what made him say that,' said Mrs Sharp in wonderment.

'Because he's an incorrigible liar.'

Mrs Sharp strove to be reasonable. 'Most kids tell lies now and again to get out of a spot of bother.'

'George tells more lies than most – mind you,' the headmistress's lips twisted with humour, 'we were all amused at the idea of George tidying, considering he's the untidiest boy in the class.'

Mrs Sharp reared up. 'Oh, is he? Well let me tell you he's tidy when he leaves the house. I make him wash his face and comb his hair every day. How the devil should I know what he gets up to when he leaves?'

'Keep calm, Mrs Sharp. I'm sure you do your best under the circumstances.'

'What circumstances?'

'Don't you work?' the headmistress asked pleasantly.

Mrs Sharp sagged. She had a presentiment of doom. Her husband had never liked her working. 'A woman's place is in the home,' he always said when any crisis arose – despite the fact that her income was a necessity.

'Yes,' she said.

'Of course,' said the headmistress, her spectacles directed towards the top of Mrs Sharp's head, 'I understand that many mothers work nowadays, but unfortunately they are producing a generation of latch-key children running wild. Far be it for me to judge the parents' circumstances, but I think a child's welfare comes first.' She smiled toothily. 'Perhaps I'm old-fashioned, but –'

'I suppose you're going to tell me a woman's place is in the home?' asked Mrs Sharp, through tight lips.

'If she has children, I would say so.'

Mrs Sharp threw caution to the wind. 'If I didn't work George wouldn't have any uniform to go to school with – '

She broke off at the entrance of an agitated tangle-haired young woman.

'I'm sorry, Miss McHare,' said the young woman, 'I didn't know you were with someone – '

'That's all right,' said the headmistress. 'What is it?'

'It's George Sharp again.'

'Dear, dear!' The headmistress braced herself while Mrs Sharp slumped.

'He was fighting, in the playground. Ken Wilson has a whopper of an eye. Sharp is outside. I was going to send him in, but if you're engaged – '

The headmistress addressed Mrs Sharp. 'You see what I mean. It just had to be George again.'

She turned to the young teacher. 'This is George's mother.'

'Good morning,' said the young teacher, without enthusiasm.

'How do you know George started it?' asked Mrs Sharp, thrusting her pale face upwards. The headmistress stiffened. She stood up and towered above Mrs Sharp like a female Gulliver. Mrs Sharp pointed her chin at a right angle in an effort to focus properly.

The headmistress ordered, 'Bring the boy in.'

George Sharp shuffled in, tall and gangling, in contrast to his hunched mother, who gave him a weak smile when he looked at her blankly.

'Now,' said the headmistress, 'I hear you've been fighting.'

George nodded.

'You know fighting is forbidden within these grounds.'

'Ken Wilson was fighting as well,' he replied hoarsely, squinting through strands of dank hair.

'Ken Wilson is a delicate boy who does not fight.'

'He kicked me,' George mumbled, his eyes swivelling down to his sandshoes.

The headmistress explained to no one in particular, 'Of course George is not above telling lies.'

Mrs Sharp rose from her chair like a startled bird. 'Listen son, did that boy kick you?'

'Yes Ma,' George said eagerly.

'Where?'

He pointed vaguely to his leg.

'Pull up your trouser.'

George did so.

'Look,' said Mrs Sharp triumphantly, 'that's a black and blue mark.'

'Looks more like dirt,' tittered the young teacher.

'Dirt is it?' Mrs Sharp rubbed the mark. George winced.

'That's sore.'

'It's a kick mark. Deny it if you can.'

'Come now,' said the headmistress, 'we're not in a courtroom. Besides, whether it's a kick mark or not doesn't prove a thing. Possibly it was done in retaliation. Frankly I don't see Ken Wilson starting it. He hasn't got the stamina.'

'Is that so?' said Mrs Sharp. 'I know Ken Wilson better than you, and he's no better than any other kid when it comes to starting fights. He's well known for throwing stones and kicking cats – '

The headmistress intervened. 'In any case this is beside the point. I brought you here to discuss George's behaviour in general, and not this matter in particular.'

'And bloody well wasted my time,' retorted Mrs Sharp.

The headmistress's mouth fell open at the effrontery. She turned to the young teacher.

'You may go now, Miss Tilly,' adding ominously to George, 'You too, Sharp. I'll deal with you later.'

George gave his mother an anguished look as he was led out.

'Don't worry,' she called to him.

The headmistress said, 'I don't know what you mean by that, because I think your son has plenty to worry about.'

Mrs Sharp stood up placing her hands on her hips. Her cheeks were now flushed.

'You know what I think – I think this is a case of persecution. I mean the way you carried on about George fighting just proves it. And all this guff about him distracting the class – well if that flibbery gibbery miss is an example of a teacher then no wonder the class is easily distracted. Furthermore,' she continued wildly before the headmistress could draw her breath, 'I'll be writing to the authorities to let them know how my son is treated. Don't think they won't be interested because all this bullying in school is getting a big write-up nowadays.'

'How dare you talk to me like that,' said the headmistress, visibly white round the nose. 'It's your son who is the bully.'

Mrs Sharp jeered, 'So now he's a bully. While you're at it is there anything else? I suppose if you had your way he'd be off to a remand home.'

'No doubt he'll get there of his own accord.'

The remark was lost on Mrs Sharp, now launched into a tirade of reprisal for all injustices perpetrated against working-class children and her George in particular. The headmistress froze in the face of such eloquence, which was eventually summed up by the final denunciation:

'So if I was you I'd hand in my notice before all this happens. Anyway you're getting too old for the job. It stands to reason your nerves are all shook up. It's a well-known fact that spinster teachers usually end cracking up and being carted off.'

The change in their complexions was remarkable. The headmistress was flushed purple with rage and Mrs Sharp was pallid with conviction.

There was a space of silence. Then the headmistress managed to say, 'Get out – before I call the janitor.'

Mrs Sharp gave a hard laugh. 'Threats is it now? Still I'm not bothered, for it seems to me you've got all the signs of cracking up right now. By the way if you lay one finger on George I'll put you on a charge.'

She flounced out of the room when the headmistress picked up the telephone, and banged the door behind her. The headmistress replaced the receiver without dialling, then sat down at the desk with her head in her hands, staring at the open notebook.

Outside Mrs Sharp joined a woman waiting against the school railings, eating crisps.

'How did you get on?' the woman asked.

Mrs Sharp rummaged in her plastic bag and brought out a packet of cigarettes. Before she shoved one into her mouth she said, 'Tried to put me in my place she did – well I soon showed her she wasn't dealing with some kind of underling – '

The woman threw the empty crisp packet on to the grass.

'What about George?'

Mrs Sharp looked bitter. 'See that boy – he's a proper devil. Wait till I get him home and I'll beat the daylights out of him. I'll teach him to get me sent for.'

Questions and thinking points

1 Look back at the first sentence and the opening paragraphs of this story. What kind of relationship is immediately established and then reinforced between the two women?

2 How exactly does Agnes Owens achieve this effect? Look closely at the way she characterises the women through dialogue and description. (Consider the women's appearance, behaviour, attitudes.)

3 By the end of the story, the roles have been reversed. This change doesn't happen instantly and implausibly, but develops subtly. Can you trace this development and note the main landmarks? Look for Mrs Sharp's shift from defence to deliberate misunderstanding; the discussion about George's credibility; Miss McHare's criticism of Mrs Sharp's values; the impact of Miss Tilly and George; why they're dismissed; and the effect this has on Mrs Sharp.

4 Read the ending of the story again. How different would the ending be if Agnes Owens had stopped at the point where the headmistress stares at the open notebook? In what way does the ending at the school railings change everything? This is called a twist ending, because we, the readers, have our expectations turned around.

5 Are there any winners in this story? (Consider all four characters.) Any losers? Does anything change?

6 The subject of the story is an encounter between two women. But what is the theme, the idea behind the story? What

prevents Mrs Sharp from siding with the headmistress, when she freely tells the woman at the railing what a devil her George is?

Now read what Agnes Owens writes about 'Getting Sent For'.

❝ The idea of writing 'Getting Sent For', which I wrote many years ago, certainly came from the fact that I myself was a mother who every year got sent for by the Headmistress of the Primary School, on account of my youngest son. This was mainly because, on occasions, he was either fighting in the playground or causing a disturbance in the class. But, unlike the mother in the story, I did not think my son was being accused unjustly. So, though the story was based on truth, I altered it to suit myself. I am sure most writers do this. Although truth can be stranger than fiction, sometimes it can be more boring, unbelievable or unsatisfactory as a piece of fiction. Anyway, that's what I did and after ten years I think this story is as valid as a situation as it was then. Let's face it, the average mother usually thinks their child is the innocent party. ❞

Creative thinking and writing

■ *Conflict is essential to this story. Write a story of your own in which two characters are in conflict. (Choose a situation which you know something about.) Don't necessarily go for the first idea but cast around, open-minded, for the one with the most potential. Try to place one character in an apparently superior position and see if you can engineer a role-reversal by the end. Go for a twist, too, if you really want to ice your cake!*

On herself and her writing

Agnes Owens

I wrote my first short story thirty odd years ago which was published in *The Scotsman*, called 'A Hopeless Case', but nothing else after that. Fifteen years ago, I joined a writing group and proceeded to write some short stories which were published in a book shared by James Kelman and Alasdair Gray called *Lean Tales*, and then I wrote some chapters about a young brickie which eventually became the short novel called *Gentlemen of the West*. This all happened nine years ago and I have been writing on and off since. Probably I would never have thought of writing anything at all if I hadn't joined a writing group.

As to satisfaction, yes I do get it when I think I've managed to write something that is worthwhile. Quite often I can waste months in writing something that I eventually discard. So for me it is not exactly easy to get satisfaction, though I did find it when my latest novel, *A Working Mother*, was published, but now that is over and done with I'll have to start writing something else in order to get more satisfaction, that is if I can.

Further reading

Gentlemen of the West (Polygon/Penguin) – a short novel
Lean Tales (Cape) – short stories, shared with James Kelman and Alasdair Gray
Like Birds in the Wilderness (Fourth Estate) – a short novel
A Working Mother (Cape, 1994) – a full-length novel

IN THE SKIP
Brian McCabe

Half a dozen bricks
are clinging to their brickness
and to the idea of being
a wall.

Drawers lean on drawers as if
their crazy staircase could recall
the time it was a kitchen cabinet.

A mattress, doubled-up, yearns
to yawn, stretch, turn over
and scratch itself where it's ripped.

Dust, yes there is dust.
And sometimes I think
my history is there in the skip:

a gap that was once for sitting on;
a piece, missing its jigsaw;
a smatter of glass, convinced
it was always meant to be a window.

I peer into the rubble, to see
what's salvageable.

Questions and thinking points

1 This poem encourages the reader to see beyond everyday
objects into 'the idea of being'. How is this way of thinking
explored in each of the first three verses?

2 'Dust, yes there is dust.' On one level, the literal one, this is a simple, factual observation. On a more complex, metaphorical level, what are the connotations of dust?

3 The poem changes after the eleventh line. What effect does the introduction of the poet's 'voice' have, and how do the three examples in the fifth verse differ from those in the first three verses?

4 Explain how the last verse connects with the first three verses, and with the fourth and fifth verses, by working, as with the dust line, on two levels.

Now read what Brian McCabe writes about 'In the Skip':

❝ Around the time I wrote 'In the Skip' I was writing a number of poems which I thought of as very simple – not simplistic, but they used a very simple vocabulary, avoiding rich, clotted language or elaborate metaphors. I was aiming at something simple, clear and statement-like in these poems, probably because I had been influenced by the styles of certain European poets like Zbigniew Herbert, Vasco Poppa and Miroslav Holub. I thought of the poems I was writing as threadbare things, taking their shape and their rhythm from the logic of the idea in the poem, from what is called the *argument* of the poem. Sometimes what the poems were about was by no means simple, so I was trying to use the simplest language to talk about difficult things. I think 'In the Skip' is a good example of this.

The poem came about when I came out of my flat in Edinburgh one day and looked into a skip full of junk in the street outside my door. It was full of old-fashioned fittings and furnishings, all worn out and broken. I was thinking I might salvage something from it I could use in my flat. Anyway, all the bits of worn-out junk looked somehow very human to me, as if they had absorbed some of the identity of the people they had belonged to. The old bits of junk spoke of weariness and desperation, but it was also their humility which spoke to me – those bricks clinging to each other, still trying to be a wall, were like people trying to work together but falling apart. So if, by trying to describe the old bits of junk, I could maybe also say something about humanity, that would be not a bad morning's work. I don't know if I succeeded in that, but to me the poem was trying to say something about the way people's history and culture can also be consigned to the skip, can be left to disintegrate, so that it becomes necessary to search among the rubble for what can be rescued, reclaimed.

5 What are the 'difficult things' that Brian McCabe is talking about in this poem?

6 The themes of the poem are waste, loss, destruction. Is the piece ultimately optimistic or pessimistic? Justify your decision.

Creative thinking and writing

■ *Why does 'In the Skip' have to be a poem? Why can it not be a short story? If you find this question tricky, think about narrative. Consider the poem in relation to Edwin Morgan's 'Little Blue Blue', which he describes as 'a fantastic story'. If you're still unsure, read the section on 'Prose logic and poetic logic' p. 15.*

■ *Avoiding skips and their contents, come up with an example of loss, waste or destruction and try to write a poem about it, connecting it to both your own life, and its own existence. You will find yourself dealing with an object, for example a ring, which has been damaged by time, and which belonged to someone you knew whose relationship with you has also been changed by time. You will be writing about the ring as an object, and as a symbol. See if you can strengthen the structure of your poem by keeping yourself out of it at first and by keeping the connection until the end.*

Look around you – here, now and afterwards. Be receptive to the possibility of creative ideas. Then give yourself the time – a morning, maybe – to see what develops.

On himself and his writing

Brian McCabe

❝ I was born in 1951, the youngest of four children. My father worked as a miner, my mother as a cook. I grew up in Bonnyrigg, King's Lynn and Falkirk, and began writing poetry shortly before leaving Falkirk High School in 1969. My poems first came to the attention of the public when they won an award in *The Scotsman*'s School Magazine Awards. As a student at Edinburgh University, I continued to develop my own writing and became involved in reading my work in public and organising readings for other writers. After leaving university, I worked in a variety of jobs before becoming a self-employed freelance writer in 1980, when I was awarded a writer's bursary by the Scottish Arts Council. I live in Edinburgh with my family. **❞**

Further reading

Spring's Witch (Mariscat Press, 1984) – poems
The Lipstick Circus (Mainstream Publishing, 1985) – short stories
One Atom to Another (Polygon, 1987) – poems
The Other McCoy (Mainstream Publishing, 1990/
   Penguin, 1991) – a novel
In a Dark Room with a Stranger (Hamish Hamilton, 1993/
   Penguin, 1995) – short stories

It is often interesting to read those writers who have influenced the work of those you admire. Brian McCabe mentions Zbigniew Herbert, Vasco Poppa and Miroslav Holub. Track them down, in translation, through libraries or bookshops.

THE MIRACULOUS CANDIDATE
Bernard MacLaverty

At the age of fourteen John began to worry about the effects of his sanctity. The first thing had been a tingling, painful sensation in the palms of his hands and the soles of his feet. But an even more alarming symptom was the night when, as he fervently prayed himself to sleep, he felt himself being lifted up a full foot and a half above the bed – bedclothes and all. The next morning when he thought about it he dismissed it as a dream or the result of examination nerves.

Now on the morning of his Science exam he felt his stomach light and woolly, as if he had eaten feathers for breakfast. Outside the gym some of the boys fenced with new yellow rulers or sat drumming them on their knees. The elder ones, doing Senior and A levels, stood in groups all looking very pale, one turning now and again to spit over his shoulder to show he didn't care. John checked for his examination card which his grandmother had carefully put in his inside pocket the night before. She had also pinned a Holy Ghost medal beneath his lapel where it wouldn't be seen and made him wear his blazer while she brushed it. She had asked him what Science was about and when John tried to explain she had interrupted him saying, 'If y'can blether as well with your pen – you'll do all right.'

One of the Seniors said it was nearly half-past and they all began to shuffle towards the door of the gym. John had been promised a watch if he passed his Junior.

The doors were opened and they all filed quietly to their places. John's desk was at the back with his number chalked on the top right-hand corner. He sat down, unclipped his fountain-pen and set it in the groove. All the desks had an empty hole for an ink-well. During the Maths exam one of the boys opposite who couldn't do any of the questions drew a face in biro on his finger and put it up through the hole and waggled it at John. He didn't seem to care whether he failed or not.

John sat looking at the wall-bars which lined the gym. The

invigilator held up a brown paper parcel and pointed to the unbroken seal, then opened it, tearing off the paper noisily. He had a bad foot and some sort of high boot which squeaked every time he took a step. His face was pale and full of suspicion. He was always jumping up suddenly as if he had caught somebody on, flicking back his stringy hair as he did so. When he ate the tea and biscuits left at the door for him at eleven his eyes kept darting back and forward. John noticed that he 'gullied', a term his grandmother used for chewing and drinking tea at the same time. When reading, he never held the newspaper up but laid it flat on the table and stood propped on his arms, his big boot balanced on its toe to take the weight off it.

'If you ever meet the devil you'll know him by his cloven hoof,' his Granny had told him. A very holy woman, she had made it her business to read to him every Sunday night from the lives of the Saints, making him sit at her feet as she did so. While she read she let her glasses slip down to the end of her long nose and would look over them every so often, to see if he was listening. She had a mole on her chin with hair like a watch-spring growing out of it. She read in a serious voice, very different to her ordinary one, and always blew on the fine tissuey pages to separate them before turning over with her trembling fingers. She had great faith and had a particular saint for every difficulty. 'St Blaise is good for throats and if you've ever lost anything St Anthony'll find it for you.' She always kept sixpence under the statue of the Child of Prague because then, she said, she'd never be without. Above all there was St Joseph of Cupertino. For examinations he was your man. Often she read his bit out of the book to John.

'Don't sit with your back to the fire or you'll melt the marrow of your bones,' and he'd change his position at her feet and listen intently.

St Joseph was so close to God that sometimes when he prayed he was lifted up off the ground. Other times when he'd be carrying plates – he was only smart enough to work in the kitchen – he would go into a holy trance and break every dish on the tiled floor. He wanted to become a priest but he was very stupid so he learned off just one line of the Bible. But here – and this was the best part of the story – when his exam came didn't God make the Bishop ask him the one line he knew and he came through with flying colours. When the story was finished his Granny always said, 'It was all he was fit for, God help him – the one line.'

The invigilator squeaked his way down towards John and flicked a pink exam paper onto his desk. John steadied it with his hand. His eyes raced across the lines looking for the familiar questions. The feathers whirlpooled almost into his throat. He panicked. There was not a single question – *not one* – he knew anything about. He tried to settle himself and concentrated to read the first question.

State Newton's Universal Law of Gravitation. Give arguments for or against the statement that 'the only reason an apple falls downwards to meet the earth instead of the earth falling upwards to meet the apple is that the earth, being much more massive exerts the greater pull.' The mass of the moon is one eighty-first, and its radius one quarter that of the earth. What is the acceleration of gravity at its surface if . . .

It was no use. He couldn't figure out what was wrong. He had been to mass and communion every day for the past year – he had prayed hard for the right questions. The whole family had prayed hard for the right questions. What sort of return was this? He suppressed the thought because it was . . . it was God's will. Perhaps a watch would lead him into sin somehow or other?

He looked round at the rest of the boys. Most of them were writing frantically. Others sat sucking their pens or doodling on their rough-work sheets. John looked at the big clock they had hung on the wall-bars with its second hand slowly spinning. Twenty minutes had gone already and he hadn't put pen to paper, he must do *something*.

He closed his eyes very tight and clenching his fists to the side of his head he placed himself in God's hands and began to pray. His Granny's voice came to him. 'The Patron Saint of Examinations. Pray to him if you're really stuck.' He saw the shining damp of his palms, then pressed them to his face. Now he summoned up his whole being, focused it to a point of white heat. All the good that he had ever done, that he ever would do, all his prayers, the sum total of himself, he concentrated into the name of the Saint. He clenched his eyes so hard there was a roaring in his ears. His finger-nails bit into his cheeks. His lips moved and he said, 'Saint Joseph of Cupertino, help me.'

He opened his eyes and saw that somehow he was above his desk. Not far – he was raised up about a foot and a half, his body still in a sitting position. The invigilator looked up from his paper and John tried to lower himself back down into his seat. But he had no control over his limbs. The invigilator came round his desk quickly and walked towards him over the coconut matting, his boot creaking as he came.

'What are you up to?' he hissed between his teeth.

'Nothing,' whispered John. He could feel his cheeks becoming more and more red, until his whole face throbbed with blushing.

'Are you trying to copy?' The invigilator's face was on a level with the boy's. 'You can see every word the boy in front of you is writing, can't you?'

'No sir, I'm not trying to . . . ' stammered John. 'I was just praying and . . . ' The man looked like a Protestant. The Ministry brought in teachers from other schools. Protestant schools. He wouldn't understand about Saints.

'I don't care what you say you were doing. I think you are trying to copy and if you don't come down from there I'll have you disqualified.' The little man was getting as red in the face as John.

'I can't sir.'

'Very well then.' The invigilator clicked his tongue angrily and walked creak-padding away to his desk.

John again concentrated his whole being, focused it to a prayer of white heat.

'Saint Joseph of Cupertino. *Get me down please*.' But nothing happened. The invigilator lifted his clip-board with the candidates' names and started back towards John. Some of the boys in the back row had stopped writing and were laughing. The invigilator reached him.

'Are you going to come down from there or not?'

'I can't.' The tears welled up in John's eyes.

'Then I shall have to ask you to leave.'

'I can't,' said John.

The invigilator leaned forward and tapped the boy in front of John on the shoulder.

'Do you mind for a moment?' he said and turned the boy's answer paper face downwards on the desk. While he was turned away John frantically tried to think of a way out. His prayer hadn't worked . . . maybe a sin would . . . the invigilator turned to him.

'For the last time I'm . . . '

'Fuck the Pope,' said John and as he did so, he plumped back down into his seat skinning his shin on the tubular frame of the desk.

'Pardon. What did you say?' asked the invigilator.

'Nothing sir. It's all right now. I'm sorry sir.'

'What *is* wrong with you boy?'

'I can't do it, sir – any of it.' John pointed to the paper. The invigilator spun it round with his finger.

'You should have thought of that some months ago . . . ' The words faded away. 'I'm very sorry. Just a minute,' he said, limping very quickly down to his desk. He came back with a white exam paper which he put in front of John.

'Very sorry,' he repeated. 'It does happen sometimes.'

John looked for the first time at the head of the pink paper. ADVANCED LEVEL PHYSICS. Now he read quickly through the questions on the white paper the invigilator had brought him. They were all there. Archimedes in his bath, properties of NaCl, allotropes of sulphur, the anatomy of the buttercup. The invigilator smiled with his spade-like teeth.

'Is that any better?' he asked. John nodded. ' . . . and if you need some extra time to make up, you can have it.'

'Thank you sir,' said John. The invigilator hunkered down beside him and whispered confidentially.

'This wee mix-up'll not go any farther than between ourselves, will it . . . ' He looked down at his clip-board. ' . . . Johnny?'

'No sir.'

He gave John a pat on the back and creaked away over the

coconut matting. John put his head down on the desk and uttered a prayer of Thanksgiving to St Joseph of Cupertino, this time making sure to keep his fervour within bounds.

Questions and thinking points

1 The main plotline here is that a boy is given the wrong exam paper, he panics, and is then given the right one. How do the religious overtones contribute to the humour? (Consider the title, the first paragraph, the character and actions of the grandmother and the invigilator, the boy's first and second reactions to the Newton question, his solution to the levitation problem, and the last sentence.)

2 Swearing is not generally encouraged in creative writing assignments. Why do you think this is? To what extent do you think the swearing is justified here? You may first like to consider this question objectively, in the context of the story and in relation to John's own character, and then subjectively, from your own personal point of view.

Now read what Bernard MacLaverty writes about 'The Miraculous Candidate':

 I remember the story came to me in an examination. I was in my late twenties and I was trying to gain admission to a university course or get a scholarship which would help me through a university course – I can't remember which. Anyway, I was doing very badly and feeling particularly stupid; none of the questions suited me and I felt I should just get up and leave. (I remember once, in my first year at secondary school, being in a similar position in a religious knowledge exam and bursting a boil on the back of my neck so that the invigilator would excuse me from the room.) But I stayed on and looked at the lines of sweat on my palms. The only strategy left seemed to be prayer and even though I was deeply sceptical I found myself remembering from my school days St Joseph of Cupertino, Patron Saint of Examinations. He was, in today's jargon, adversely gifted and as a child was known as 'the gaper'; he was also liable to levitations – suspensions or flights in the air. (Since writing the story I have found out, much to my amusement, that he is also the Patron Saint of air travellers.) In the time left to me I jotted down the outline of the story on a blank examination booklet.

I also remembered the man who invigilated when I sat my Senior Certificate. (The verb 'sat' is good in this context.) He had a limp and a boot which squeaked as he paced continually up and down the coconut matting spread to protect the maple floor of the gym.

My wife, Madeline, had told me the sad story of sitting her first year exams in Celtic at the University. Unable to answer hardly any of the questions, she wept and was led from the hall. She was advised to return and do as much as she was able. Afterwards, when conducting a post mortem with friends, she found she had been given the Honours Celtic paper by mistake.

I knew the examination in the story should be a scientific one – religion and science sometimes don't sit too comfortably together – but I was delighted to find an actual A-level physics question on gravity. It also included the word 'apple', with its Adam and Eve associations and its connections with 'original sin'; and the word 'earth' which is often the bedfellow of 'heaven'.

The thing I like in the story is the refusal of the invigilator to admit that anything odd is going on and that all he is dealing with is a blatant attempt to copy.

Creative thinking and writing

Whereas Brian McCabe, in 'In the Skip', looks beyond objects, Bernard MacLaverty gathers and selects material from relevant realities and then fictionalises them into a taut and coherent whole. Both these processes require an open mind, an ability to use your own and others' experiences, and to connect them in an artistically satisfying way.

'The Miraculous Candidate' has a chronological storyline, with two problems and two solutions, all interlinked. John's first problem is that he can't answer any questions on the exam paper. His anguish leads to the second problem of being stuck in mid-air. The solution to the second problem is to swear, which leads to the solution of the first problem – he gets the right exam paper. Be aware of this chain-reaction method of structuring a piece of writing. It is easily managed because it is chronological.

'Getting Sent For' (p. 39) uses a similar chronological structure but 'two fragments' (p. 79), 'Scarab' (p. 150) and 'The Travelling Poet' (p. 95) diverge from this. 'two fragments' has two anecdotes, which are told with a chronological structure, but they are embedded within a whole, which is fragmentary until the last three lines draw everything together. 'Scarab' begins in the recent past, shifts to a generation earlier, then finishes in the present. This allows us to start and finish with the main characters, and the flashback middle section adds poignancy and irony to the ending. 'The Travelling Poet' does have a loosely chronological structure, but the story diverges into the thoughts and anecdotes of the narrator. By the end, the story has shifted from being about the poet, to being about the narrator, who has come to a new level of self-awareness through his contact with the travelling poet.

■ *Look closely at the way Bernard MacLaverty characterises the invigilator throughout the story – through dialogue, physical details and mannerisms. (Notice the man's symbolic role as the devil.) Look, too, at the second paragraph, and see how even the briefest details manage to characterise John and the older boys.*

■ *See if you can write a story – nothing to do with school, religion or examinations – in which your central character has a problem, with a complicated solution. Craft your piece, and try to set up the ending at the beginning, as Bernard MacLaverty does in his story. Also try to use unusual but relevant detail to create vivid characters.*

This is not the kind of writing you can do straight away. You will have to think, make notes, score things out, and rewrite and struggle a bit. But the more work you put in, the better the results will be, if not in this story, then in future ones.

Use your life and other people's life experiences as inspiration. Take real events, select bits, connect them, make up other bits and see if you can end up with a good story. It's very difficult to make things up completely, and recording truth can be very boring. Creative writing swoops and swings freely between truth and fiction and weaves a persuasive spell.

On himself and his writing

Bernard MacLaverty

'I was born in Belfast (14 September 1942). In 1975 I moved to Scotland with my family. I have had various jobs, the last of which was a teacher of English. After living for a time in Edinburgh and on the Isle of Islay, I am now in Glasgow. I have published four collections of stories and two novels, and written versions of these for other media – radio, television and the cinema.

I began writing in my last year at school. Bad poetry. I didn't set out to write bad poetry, it's just the way it came out. I liked everything about words – their sound, the multiple meanings, their rhythms when strung together. I even liked reading *Roget's Thesaurus*. Twenty different ways to say the same thing.

But it took a long time before I finished anything. I was always writing fragments of things. And copying other people's ways of writing (Kafka and Joyce and Gerard Manley Hopkins). Then I wrote a story, *'The Exercise'*, which was in my own voice about a place and people I knew. It was accepted by the BBC and that got me started.

When I was young I used to like playing farms – setting out the toy animals, ducks on a round mirror pond, and the farmer and his wife, maybe one day face to face, the next day with their backs to each other. Making up a world. I think I go on writing because it is the same kind of play activity.'

Further reading

Secrets and Other Stories (Blackstaff Press, 1977)
Lamb (Cape/Blackstaff Press, 1980) – a novel
A Time to Dance and Other Stories (Cape/Blackstaff Press, 1982)
Cal (Cape/Blackstaff Press, 1983) – a novel
The Great Profundo and Other Stories (Cape/Blackstaff Press, 1987)
Walking the Dog and Other Stories (Cape/Blackstaff Press, 1994)

You might like to find out more about the three writers whom Bernard MacLaverty mentions above:

Franz Kafka (1883–1924): 'Metamorphosis' (a short story), *The Trial* and *The Castle* (both novels).
James Joyce (1882–1941): *Dubliners* (short stories), *A Portrait of the Artist as a Young Man* (autobiography), *Ulysses* and *Finnegans Wake* (landmark novels in literary innovation).
Gerard Manley Hopkins (1844–89): *Poems*.

CLOCKWORK
Daniel O'Rourke

Broken clocks and watches were my father's hobby
Killing time, he'd say, no irony intended,
So grandfathers loitered dumbstruck in our lobby
Hands salaaming as if begging to be mended.

Testimonial tokens of lifetimes on the job
Added to his pile their grateful mollusc gape
Stammering snuff-stained waistcoat fobs
Tick corrected by puff and scrape.

Eyeglass squinched, he'd read the auguries
Pronounce and whistle, arrange his tiny tools
Wind the watch until we'd hear it wheeze
Teaching me to prod among the cogs and spools

Though my cag-handedness loomed larger through his glass
He didn't mind his skill not passing on
It's a stoic's pastime, letting time pass,
He knew with quartz and plastic the need was gone

Now his hands are slow and he's lost his spring
His face is scuffed by the emery-paper years
But he can value a clock by its pendulum swing
Or the watch by the tact of the tick that he hears

And on Sundays sometimes we'd both repair
To smile at every deep-voiced mantel chime
So many hunched gloamings recalled quiet there
My father and I keeping perfect time.

Questions and thinking points

1 Why is it appropriate that this poem should have a regular verse form, and regular rhyme? Why do you think the rhythm is less regular?

2 Daniel O'Rourke has had fun playing with language and ideas. Consider the title and his use of puns, metaphors and personification. How does he blur the differences between timepieces and people? In what order does this happen?

3 Explain how the relationship between father and son changes. How many levels of meaning can you find in the last line?

4 Look at 'In the Skip' by Brian McCabe (p. 49). Compare the two poems, thinking about subject matter, form, the role of the poet and the point at which he enters the poem. Look also at the conclusion each poet draws from the two lines of thought developed in each poem.

Now read what Daniel O'Rourke writes about 'Clockwork':

❝ With this simple wee poem, what you see is what you get; a real memory, only slightly retouched in the telling. The sudden, rapt work of a winter Sunday teatime that seemed to take only a minute or two longer to write than it does to read. Being a fairly fluent rhymer, I've tended to be suspicious of that facility. 'Clockwork' is one of the very few rhyming poems I have produced. What was so capriciously given, came with its own built-in rhythm – a sort of childlike tick-tock that seems appropriate. The thought of publication never really occurred to me although I'm delighted that the editor of this book liked it enough to copy it out and include it here. The 'poem' seemed too naive, too sentimental, one of those, 'Aaaaaagh!' greetings card efforts. But I suppose it has a good memory for detail and it's sincere in its simple-heartedness. That's how it was and how we were. I'd have been in my late twenties when I wrote it, conscious as I went along that because of my mechanical ineptitude, this was *my* clockwork. Poetry is something I do, more than a hobby but less than a full-time job. Dad was still alive when I wrote 'Clockwork' and I was aware at the time of an elegiac note creeping in. It didn't feel morbid however. Now, three years after his death, it ticks away at the back of my mind, compensating in some way for the fact that his handiwork ticks on, on other people's mantelpieces and wrists. Mind you, on my wrist, there's an old-fashioned wind-up watch, Russian, stainless steel, solid not flashy. Runs like. . . .

Creative thinking and writing

In both 'In the Skip' and 'Clockwork', a situation, and a way of thinking about it is introduced. Then a second element, the poet's involvement, is brought in. The writers manage to end their poems by connecting both lines of thought in a concise pun. This effect can be formulated as $1 + 1 = 3$: the two parts adding up to a conclusion with extra impact.

■ *See if you can write a poem which develops in this way. It may not be an easy exercise, but the thinking practice won't go to waste. You need one idea or line of thought to begin with. Choose an activity – nothing to do with time – and then introduce 'yourself', with a different or conflicting attitude. See if you can come up with an ending which links to both parts. You will have to dare to be vulnerable on this. Your poem will probably not fall into place first time, but stick with it, sleep on it and, if you give it breathing space, it'll come to life.*

■ *'Clockwork' is a poem about relationships linked through a common activity. Choose someone you love, or loved. Think of an activity which you both shared, perhaps with varying degrees of skill or enjoyment, and see if you can write a poem in honour of this relationship.*

■ *The current fashion is for free verse, which is poetry where rhyme, rhythm, line length and stanza length do not conform to a regular, repeating pattern. Why do you think this is? Crafting language into regular rhyme is a skill. And there can be a lot of satisfaction in trying to keep the meaning while at the same time avoiding jingly rhyme. See if you can write some rhyming couplets. Then try a four-line verse, with a rhyme on the second and fourth lines. Then try what Daniel O'Rourke has done, and rhyme first and third, second and fourth.*

On himself and his writing

Daniel O'Rourke

When I started to write poetry I was a bit sceptical. I was 14 or thereabouts and puberty, the guitar and the urge to write all seemed to coincide and feed off each other. It was partly embarrassment that converted the poetic drive into the more socially acceptable (in the 70s) song-writing. Poetry with a capital P came back in my 20s when I began to publish. I'm a minor poet and a sporadic one – an inspiration man rather than a set-hours writer. For influence, I look most to America and Ireland. If you haven't already, do check out Muldoon, Paulin, Durcan and O'Hara. I'll gain nothing from the comparison, I'm afraid, but I console myself with the thought that one of these days a really *good* poem might just happen along.

Further reading

You will find more of Daniel O'Rourke's poetry in the following books:

Second Cities (Vennel Press, 1991)
Dream State (editor and contributor) (Polygon, 1994)

If you find rhyming poetry enjoyable, you might like to look at the poetry of Thomas Hardy, who was constantly experimenting with verse forms and rhyme. He was writing in the early decades of this century.

Tony Harrison is a modern poet whose rhyming poetry is also well worth tracking down.

THE OLD WOMAN'S REEL

Valerie Gillies

She is at the small deep window
looking through and out:
the Aran islands, rock and seawater,
lie all about.
A face strong in poverty's hauteur
is hers, then and now.

Being a young woman in Flaherty's film
'Man of Aran',
she nearly drowned in the undertow
by the boat where she ran.
He kept on filming even though
he thought her dead on the rockrim.

A body plaited by water twine
they carried ashore:
partnered in the ocean's set dance
by two men or more.
The sea had had its chance
to peel her off by the shoreline.

Now in her great old age
toothless and tough,
the island music still delights her:
one dance is not enough.
The tunes of a people poor and cut off there
have a special power to engage.

Drawn upright, her stiff bones
already dancing,

she spins, not on one foot
but on her stick, tap-balancing.
While to one side like a pliant offshoot
a little girl mimics her, unbeknown.

Questions and thinking points

1 How soon were you aware that this poem has a regular rhyming scheme? Look closely at the rhymes. Why has Valerie Gillies chosen to rhyme the poem? Why has she also kept the rhymes subtle? What do they add to the poem?

2 The poem is about the past and the present. At what point does it also describe the future?

3 In the third verse, the poet offers us some images. What does 'a body plaited by the water twine' make you see? What do you understand by 'the ocean's set dance' and 'to peel her off by the shoreline'?

Now read what Valerie Gillies writes about 'The Old Woman's Reel':

You might look at this old woman who's dancing and think, 'She's old, too old to dance', but the next moment she ups and joins in the reel with everybody else. She's born with that rhythm, like you are if you're making a poem. I've seen women like her in the Highlands and Islands, at the same dance where their children and grandchildren are enjoying themselves.

She is a woman in her nineties, who lives on the Aran islands off the west coast of Ireland. In the 1930s, when she was young, the famous film director Robert Flaherty arrived there, to make a drama and documentary about the islanders before their traditional way of life disappeared. He had already made films, such as *Nanook of the North* about Eskimos and *Elephant Boy* about Indian mahouts. He always made films on location in remote areas, under tremendous difficulties. On Aran the men fished in dangerous seas. He filmed the men and this woman together, trying to put one of the boats to sea, through rough waves, just as they did every day. Even though two of the men were drowned that morning, he went on filming. The woman was dragged ashore and survived. She is a survivor of those hard times, and glad to be alive.

Today she sits at the window of her crofthouse, looking out to sea and to a shore where every inlet and bay and cliff has a name and every rock is a place where her people have gathered shellfish or tied up a boat. If there's a dance, she joins in, using her stick to help her keep going. Her little great-granddaughter copies her dance behind her back: past and present are dancing together into the future.

Some of these details I observed on a TV programme about the history of film-making. I don't usually write poems inspired by watching the telly. I came to write the poem later, while listening to a friend playing a reel on the harp. She began by knocking four taps on the wooden soundboard, to give the beat of the tune. That knock hit the mark for me. My mind flashed on the picture of the old woman dancing, her stick tapping the rhythm, her great energy sweeping her away into the reel. That sound took me everywhere: to the Aran islands, to the room filled with dancers, to the wild seas outside, to write on the waves.

I think this poem does what it's meant to do. You can see the old woman all right, and you can hear the sound of her dance. These islanders have all the best tunes.

Recently the artist Will Maclean did a drawing to go with the poem, showing the type of *currach* or fishing boat which is the right one for the Aran islands. He put a banner above the boat, and on it you can make out the figure of the old woman. Will was a sailor and a fisherman himself so if he likes the poem I'm happy with it.

Creative thinking and writing

As with many other writers, Valerie Gillies' inspiration came as a result of connecting separate sources of experience. The TV documentary on Flaherty, plus four taps on the soundboard of a harp, flared into this poem. But only because Valerie Gillies was receptive to this possibility. She couldn't have made it happen, but she was able to respond when it did. Keep your own mind and senses open – the way you, as an individual, react to anything and everything can be inspiring.

■ *Think of someone you know, or have observed closely (on screen or in reality) and whose life is very different from yours. Write either a poem or a prose portrait of them, highlighting these differences.*

■ *Music, too, can be a catalyst for a piece of writing, and poetry is akin to song. Valerie Gillies finds inspiration for her poems in working with musicians. If there is a piece of music or a song that arouses strong feelings in you, see if you can channel them into a poem or a story.*

On herself and her writing

Valerie Gillies

■ The first time I made a poem was when I was fourteen, out walking, and writing it down later. That's the way I usually work today. I'm on a journey and someday I hope to get to what I really want to say. Meanwhile, poems are maps and sea charts, accurate discoveries.

At home the puppy chewed the cover off my book and my children argued, so now I write in the bacon roll café at Perth bus station early on a winter morning, or alone in the woods, on my front doorstep, in trains, at the counter in Luca's ice-cream shop, by a river with my feet on a boulder in the water. On this path I'm just a pair of boots and a pencil. Going out to write is the perfect life, for me.

I am a poet who often works with visual artists and musicians. I also write for television and radio, and have been writer in residence in schools, in a college of art, with the Borders Festival, and with Mid- and East Lothian District Councils. ▶

Further reading

You can find more of Valerie Gillies' poems in the following books:

Each Bright Eye (Canongate, 1977)
Bed of Stone (Canongate, 1984)
Tweed Journey (Canongate, 1989)
The Chanter's Tune (Canongate, 1990)
The Ringing Rock (Scottish Cultural Press, 1995)

TWO FRAGMENTS
Janice Galloway

I remember two things in particular about my father. He had ginger hair and two half fingers on one hand. The ring finger and the middle one fastened off prematurely at the knuckle, like the stumpy tops of two pink pork links, but smoother. They were blown off during the war. This was a dull sort of thing, though; my mother had another story that suited my child-need far better.

It started with the usual, your daddy in the pub. I could've had a mint of money today if he hadn't been a drinker by the way. Anyway he'd been in there all night and he came out the pub for the last bus up the road, but by the time he staggered to the stop he was just in time to see it going away without him. He chased it but it wasn't for stopping. He'd missed it. There was nothing for it but to start walking. He had to go along past Piacentinis on the corner and that was where he smelt the chips. It wasn't all that late yet and they were still open. The smell of the chips was a great thing on a cold night and with all the road still to go up and he just stood there for a wee while sniffing up the warm chips smell. It made him that hungry he thought he had to go in and get some, so he counted all the loose change in his pockets and with still having the bus fare he just had enough. He was that drunk though he dropped all the money and he had to crawl about all over the road to get it all back because he needed every penny to get the chips. That took him a wee while. And by the time he finally got in, Mrs Piacentini was just changing the fat and so he had to wait. That was all right but the smell of the chips was making him hungry by this time. Just when he was about to get served, a big polisman came in and asked for his usual four bags and because he was in a hurry and he was a regular he got served the chips that were for your daddy. So by the time he was watching the salt and vinegar going on to his bag, his mouth was going like a watering can. He was starving. The minute he got out into the street with them, he tore open the bag and started eating them with his fingers, stuffing them into his mouth umpteen

79

at a time and swallowing them too fast. He thought they were the best chips he had ever tasted. He was that carried away eating them that it wasn't till he went to crumple up the empty bag and fling it away he saw the blood. When he looked over his shoulder there was a trail of it all the way up the road from Piacentinis. He was that hungry he'd eaten two of his fingers for chips with salt and vinegar.

My granny had a glass eye. She was a fierce woman. A face like a white gingernut biscuit and long, long grey hair. She smoked a clay pipe. And she had this glass eye.

My grandfather was a miner, and the miners got to take the bad coal, the stuff with the impurities the coal board weren't allowed to sell. She built up the fire one day and was bashing a big lump of this impure coal with the poker when it exploded and took her eye out. So there was another story about that. Again, it was my mothers: I was much too feart for my granny to ask her anything.

Your granny could be awful cruel sometimes. She drowned cats. She drowned the kittens and if the cats got too much she drowned them as well. There was one big tom in particular used to come up the stairs and leave messes in the close. Gad. Right outside your door and everything. Stinking the place out. I don't like tom cats and neither did your granny. She got so fed up with the rotten smell and its messes that one day she decided she was going to get rid of it. So she laid out food and when it came to eat the food she was going to sneak up on it with a big bag. It was that suspicious, watching her the whole time while it was eating: your granny staring at the cat and the cat staring back. It was eating the food in the one corner and your granny was hovering with the bag in the other. High Noon. Anyway, she waited for her minute and she managed to get it. Not right away, though. It saw her and jumped, but it went the wrong way and got itself in a corner and she finally managed to get the bag over it. By the time she got into the kitchen, with the cat struggling in the bag, she was a mass of scratches. The cat was growling through the bag and trying to get its claws through at her again, so she held up the bag and shook it to show it who was the boss. Then she didn't know what to do next, till she clapped eyes on the boiler.

A wee, old-fashioned boiler like a cylinder thing on wee legs with a lid at the top. She got a string and tied up the top of the bag and then she dropped the cat right into the boiler drum. It was empty, of course. She was going to keep it in there till the boys came back (that's your uncle Sammy and uncle Alec) and get one of them to take it to the tip and choke it or something. She was fed up with it after all that wrestling about. She got on with her work in the kitchen, and as she was working about she could hear the cat banging about in the boiler the whole time, trying to get out, while she was getting on with the dinner and boiling up kettles of water for the boys coming home for their wash. When they got in from their work, the first thing they did was get a wash: there was no baths in the pit and they never sat down to their tea dirty. Your granny wouldn't let them. So they came right into the kitchen when they got home and the first thing they noticed was this thumping coming out of the boiler. Alec says to her what the hell's that mother and she tells them about the tom cat. Just at that the thing starts growling as if it's heard them and our Sammy says I hope you don't think I'm touching that bloody thing, listen to it. And he starts washing at the sink and laughing like it was nothing to do with him. Even our Alec wouldn't go and lift the lid. So she got quite annoyed and rolled her sleeves up to show them the scratches to tell them she wasn't feart for it and she would do it herself. So after she'd gave them their tea, she got them out the kitchen so she could get on with it.

She had thought what she was going to do. First, she got two big stones from the coalhouse and the big coal bucket from the top of the stair. She put the bricks at the boiler side and filled the big bucket with cold water at the sink. The cat had stopped making so much noise by this time so it was probably tired. This would be a good time. She got the washing tongs, the big wooden things for lifting out the hot sheets after they'd been boiled, and went over to the boiler, listening. Then she flung back the lid, reached in quick with the tongs and pulled the bag out before the cat knew what was happening. The minute it was out the drum, though, it starts thrashing about again and your granny drops the bag and runs over to the sink for the pail, heaves it over to the boiler and pours the whole lot in. She filled it right up nearly to the top. The bag was scuffling about the floor so she waited till it went still again. Then when it had stopped moving, she gets hold of it with the tongs quick and plonks it straight into the water, banging the lid down shut and the bricks on top.

She went straight into the living room to build up the fire and tell the boys she'd managed fine without them, quite pleased with herself. She would just leave the cat in the boiler till the next morning to be sure it was drowned and get the bucket men to take it away. Sammy was a bit offended. He said she was a terrible woman but they didn't do anything about the poor bloody cat so they were just as bad. There was no noise in the kitchen when they went for a wash before they went to their bed. It was a shame.

Well it was still the same thing the next morning when your granny went in to light the kettle. Nothing coming out the boiler. That was fine. She got me and Tommy away to the school and your uncle Alec and Sammy were away to the pit and our Lizzie was out as well. So that was her by herself and she started getting the place ready for the disposal of the body. She put big sheets of newspaper all round the floor and got the tongs ready. It would be heavy. She shifted one of the bricks off the boiler lid and listened to make sure. Nothing. She shifted the other one off and lifted up the lid. There was a hellish swoosh and the cat burst out the boiler, soaking to the bone, its eyes sticking right out its head. It must've fought its way out the bag and been swimming in there all night, paddling and keeping just its nose above the water, and the minute it saw the light when your granny lifted the lid, it just threw itself up. It shot straight at her face and took her eye out just like that. Your granny in one corner of the kitchen, with the eye in another and the tom cat away like buggery down the stairs.

Fingers for the army.
An eye for the coal board.
A song and a dance for the wean.

Questions and thinking points

1 The voice narrating this story changes between paragraph one and paragraph two. Try to define as precisely as you can the differences between the two voices. Consider syntax, vocabulary, the degree of personality coming through, the purpose of each voice, the pace.

2 Why is there no need for inverted commas in paragraph two, despite the change of speaker?

3 Why has Janice Galloway chosen to embed within the text the words spoken by Alec and Sammy on p. 81? How would the appearance of the story alter if this spoken passage were to be laid out conventionally? Why do we have conventions about direct speech layout? Are they always necessary? Are they ever necessary?

4 Do the last three lines of the story turn Janice Galloway's piece into more than 'two fragments'? (Compare this ending with the endings of 'In the Skip', p. 49, and 'Clockwork', p. 67. Comment on the importance of tying up loose ends, in both prose and poetry.)

Now read what Janice Galloway writes about 'two fragments':

> I'm not sure 'ideas for stories', as something separate to just ideas, exist. Everybody has ideas, things that pop into their heads and they don't know where from. 'Ideas for stories' are no different, though the writing down of any idea usually forces it to change. It forces it to refine and define itself accurately so other people can share it and turn it into something for themselves. 'two fragments' was really two stories my mother used to tell me when I was wee. They stuck, hard. Reasons are not hard to find.
>
> My mother was forty when she had me. I remember her as an over-busy, volatile and tired woman. She worried a lot about money and the house being clean. She

didn't spend a lot of time playing or telling stories. When she did, therefore, it was particularly memorable, not just for its rarity but also because she was very, very good at it.

Secondly, ours was not a close family: in fact I never used the word 'family' of them at all. Aunties and uncles would send Christmas presents or cards or, now and again, turn up on the doorstep and come in for their tea if there was a funeral, or worse, a wedding. That was it. As far as my mother and father were concerned, the marriage was profoundly unhappy, so even though they separated when I was very wee and he died a few years after – when I was, say, five or six – I remember only tension, anger and fear between them. Stories that suggested some other kinds of relationships might be possible were therefore very meaningful to me. In particular, any words that offered me a sense of connection to the dead, virtually unknown man, were very precious – no matter how surreal or strange.

Simply, then, these were my mother's stories. I wrote them in her voice because they were hers. They came out in more or less the order you see on the page, only words and phrases, syntax and punctuation were altered time and again till I felt it flowed more like the natural rhythm of my mother's speech. Now, I don't like the wee intrusions from an 'authorial' perspective: I find them a bit more arch and self-conscious than the writer I am now is comfortable with. I think I put them in first time round because I was just beginning writing and didn't have the confidence to fling the very notion of smooth, all-knowing authorial voice to the bin which I have now. Anyway. You live and learn. If I was going to do it again, I'd just let my memory of my mother's voice (a perfect pig to try and recreate, by the way: trying to get how she constructed her sentences, their vocabulary, rhythm and pace right) get on with it. That's the most important thing I've learned as a writer: trying hard not to be scared how it turns out, being as truthful as possible and just getting on with it. I would, however, retain the three lines at the end: they are me, which is where the whole thing ends.

Creative thinking and writing

■ *Janice Galloway is balancing apparent truth and fiction. The 'truth' of the lost fingers and eye is told in one way; the fiction of the lost fingers and eye is told in another. Which do you find more real? More convincing?*

■ *Stretch your fiction wings with the following exercise: think of creating a character with an injury or disability (eyes and fingers should not be involved). He or she can be based on truth or completely made up. Give a mundane reason as the 'true' cause, then concoct another explanation, which is fantastic but plausible. Think how you can connect the two in a piece of writing (no parent-to-child tales allowed). Consider the relative merits of writing your piece in the first person or the third person. Either way you are creating a character who can't bear to admit to the world the undramatic truth of his or her situation.*

■ *Janice Galloway talks about the power of her mother's story-telling. In what way has this become her inheritance? Do you have a similar inheritance?*

■ *We tend to write more formally than we speak. (We tend to be encouraged in this.) Yet the impact of conversational narration can be powerful, as is evident here (and in Alison Kermack's 'A Wee Tatty' p. 118), where the story and the way it is told enhance each other. As Janice Galloway says, it isn't easy to make such a narrative effective and apparently effortless.*

Try writing a story in a conversational style. You may want to use unfinished sentences, repetition, informal language and syntax (or sentence structure). You'll find it easier if you choose to retell one single dramatic incident.

On herself and her writing

Janice Galloway

' I was born in Ayrshire. I write because it lets me be my own boss and it allows me to talk to hundreds of people I will never meet. In a strange way, it gives me company.

I wrote when I was very wee, then stopped: only essays at school. I started again when I was 28 because I was very lonely and also skint: an advert for a story-writing competition gave me the idea to write down a dream I'd had. I didn't win the competition but was asked along as an also-ran to the presentation of the person who did. Someone I met there not only bought the one I'd written but asked me to write more. I've been doing it ever since. ' I have one son who was born in 1992.

Further reading

The Trick is to Keep Breathing (Minerva) – a novel
Blood (Minerva) – short stories
Foreign Parts (Vintage, 1995) – a novel

JOY
G. F. Dutton

Twentyseven bullfinches
in one week
of sun

visited the blossom –
so sparse
now the years

close in – of my cherry trees
from Japan. They enjoyed
each opening bud

as much as I did, not
for the whiteness
not for food

but the delight
of ripping them out
and throwing them down, a circle of white

distressing the grass
under each tree. Pure
anarchy, sheer

destruction. There was something about them
misusing the sun
for private joy

that offended my sense
of our common inheritance. And must have been why
each day, I shot them.

Twentyseven bullfinches
in one week of sun. The best,
almost, with that particular gun.

Questions and thinking points

1 Do you find this poem shocking? Do you think it is G. F.
Dutton's intention that you be shocked? *Should* you be
shocked?

2 In this poem, G. F. Dutton is making a pattern from
interconnecting ideas. Explain this as fully as you can, with
reference to joy and destruction in relation to both the
bullfinches and the poet.

Now read what G. F. Dutton writes about 'Joy':

❮ *The poem describes* the reactions of an old man who sees
his precious cherry-blossom trees (the usual garden ones
of Japanese origin) being stripped of flowers by flocks of
bullfinches (exuberant pests of orchards and country
gardens). He has only a few more springs left in this life
('the years close in') for seeing his blossoms (therefore so
sparse for him now), and in a self-righteous rage he shoots
the birds.

   He feels a complicated mixture of emotions –
excitement with spring, pleasure in the blossoms, dismay
at their destruction, anger at the bullfinches, sorrow for
killing them, satisfaction at still being able to shoot
straight.

   How did I come to write the poem? I underwent a similar
experience and suffered – as most people would – a

moral confusion. The only way to restore order was to set the mix of emotions down (like an angry cat) at arm's length – distance it – and channel the energy into a disciplined form which would preserve its intensity and clarify its moment of insight.

How to set it down – this cross-symmetrical interplay of delight and destruction shared by gardener and bullfinches? This particular example of the seasonal violence fed by an impassive sun? I could have tried to analyse the whole complex interaction in prose. But the picture shone in my imagination, stark and clear as spring sunlight. I chose lean economical verse to reproduce that. The Form then decided itself after a few false starts, the Content flowed in irresistibly, and the hard work limited itself to ensuring the presentation was 'stark and clear'.

Three-line stanzas reflect the mechanically recurrent appetites of the seasons; variable line lengths and stresses within them reproduce the wrestling tensions; rhyme and assonance hold the narrative together and tune it to dominant note or suggestive discord. The first 4 stanzas narrate quietly, the 5th introduces dissonance; 7 and 8 progress from indignation to self-justifying savagery, the last line of 8 snapping shut with 'shot them' (the first climactic phrase), tightening the mild 'about them'. The final stanza repeats the idyllic introduction, but now the 27 are dead in the sun; its last line, the second climax, admits present (and previous!) gratification at the skilful despatch of competitors. The title thus presents the relativity of 'Joy'.

Yet the poem is compassionate, not ironical. Gardener, bullfinches, all life, must fight for the crop, even if it is one of pleasure. Compassion is implicit, suppressed. To state it would defuse the poetic package: whose energy first shocks the reader, then drives him to recognise the source of his shock – his own moral discomfort; the only evidence of morality in the universe, and available to *H. sapiens* – through evolutionary chance or divine purpose –

only at moments of insight. The business of Art is to record moments of insight, not preach. I have tried to record one in 'Joy': but poems have (or should have) a life of their own: beware of subsequent sermons by the begetter! – who does not so much beget as transmit. For 'creative' writing is, I think, a process of communicating the insight effectively to oneself and maybe others. A technique of communication can be taught, but you can't teach anyone to 'receive' these inexplicable moments of insight – only to be ready to record them as efficiently as possible in a personal idiom.

What do I think of it now? I still like it. It still communicates to me whatever insight the experience afforded at the time. I judge it to be verse tuned much higher than low-energy prose, but not tuned to the highest poetic intensity: for it *could* be almost fully reproduced *in* prose (though then requiring more space and considerable skill), which indicates it carries insufficient of the 'Incommunicable by Prose' requirement that characterises the richest poetry. Poetic logic supplements and can supplant prose logic, and this verse is probably overburdened with the prose variety: which perhaps makes it more immediately readable for teaching purposes!

'Reality' and the final product? Whether there were 7, 27 or 107 bullfinches, whether the trees possessed Japanese, American or Scottish genes, or whether the episode occurred at all, is no part of the poetic reality – which is the only reality of this particular experience of spring. However, since these notes are supposed to pry into the accidental happening behind it: 27 – yes; Japanese – no, the trees were Scottish wild geans, precious because at their altitudinal limit for flowering; gun – no, a rifle . . . Trivia like these fill out a prose account, but would distractingly clutter any presentation in verse.

3 'The business of Art is to record moments of insight, not preach.' To what extent do you think creative writing is affected when preaching is the driving force? For example, if the poem said bullfinches should all be shot, or that shooting birds is cruel, what effect would this have?

Creative thinking and writing

G. F. Dutton talks of moments of insight; Iain Crichton Smith talks of gifts; Valerie Gillies talks of the catalytic beats on the harp soundboard. These moments of intensity are there if you are open to receiving them. It's a bit like putting crumbs out for the birds and waiting for them to arrive. They might not come. You might miss them. But you might be lucky. You might even destroy them.

■ *It's very useful to be able to draw the distinction between poetic logic and prose logic. (See the introductory section on this subject on p. 15.) Read G. F. Dutton's penultimate paragraph again.*
   Then consider other poems you know well and work out where you would place them on the scale of poetic intensity, using their suitability to be reproduced in prose as your criterion. (Compare, for example, Little Blue Blue, p. 32, and 'Second Infancy', p. 138.)

■ *You can also do the reverse, and imagine how well a short story might work as a poem – 'Getting Sent For' (p. 39)? 'two fragments' (p. 79)?*

■ *Choose a controversial subject about which you feel very strongly. Write a short 'preaching' prose piece in which you present your opinion as forcefully as possible.*
   Then, taking the same subject, see if you can write a piece containing neither censure nor opinion. Try to craft a pattern of ideas and language around the subject. This will be difficult, but it will open up your mind to the difference between putting opinions first and putting creativity – or Art – first.

On himself and his writing

G. F. Dutton

' Born of Anglo-Scottish parentage in 1924, I have been exploring since I was let out of the nest. Explorations include science, the arts, mountaineering, ski-touring, wildwater swimming, 'marginal' horticulture and forestry; and writing about them is just one more exploration. In the course of all this, I have travelled most of the globe from a Scottish hillside base, giving international talks on research medical science, and – apart from scientific ones – publishing several books, e.g. prose: *Swimming Free*, *The Ridiculous Mountains*, *Nothing So Simple As Climbing*; verse: *Camp One* and *Squaring the Waves*, which won prizes from the Scottish Arts Council, and *The Concrete Garden*, a Poetry Society Recommendation. An invited exploration linking this verse with marginal gardening, *Harvesting the Edge*, has just been published. I regard my non-scientific writing – which is perhaps edged with the passionate austerities of Scotland, urban or otherwise – as primarily for my own information; and the publishing of it, with considerable reservations . . . '

Further reading

You can find more of G. F. Dutton's poems in the following books:

Camp One (Macdonald, 1978)
Squaring the Waves (Bloodaxe Books, 1986)
The Concrete Garden (Bloodaxe Books, 1991)
Harvesting the Edge (Menard Press, 1995)

THE TRAVELLING POET
Iain Crichton Smith

One autumn day he stopped at my door. He said he was on a sponsored walk to raise money for a boy who needed medical treatment in America. He was also a poet and as he travelled, he read his poems in pubs, halls. He sold copies of them to pay for his lodgings.

He sat in the living room and took out a bag with some of the booklets that he had had published at his own expense. There were also letters from prominent people: 'Lord X thanks you for letting him see the enclosed but is sorry that he is not able to contribute to your appeal.' 'As you will understand Lady X has many demands on her resources and is sorry that she can only send two pounds at this time.'

His poems were bad. There was also a children's story about a fox which was not much better. He found out that I was a poet and asked for my opinion. I was hypocritical as usual.

It turned out that he had been in prison and that was where he had begun to write. His father had been a crane driver; his mother had been an alcoholic. He himself had been a heavy drinker but had according to himself stopped.

'When I was young,' he said, 'we were very poor. We used to beg for clothes. I have seen myself wearing girls' clothes.'

Imagine that, I thought, girls' clothes.

His wife had left him and gone to America.

'I used to be quite violent when I was young but not any more. I was in prison a few times.' This long journey to raise funds for the boy was in a way a rehabilitation for him.

He had cuttings and photographs from various local papers, with headlines such as the following: 'Ex-Convict Raises Money for Charity Mission'. And so on. He was very proud of these cuttings, and of his letters on headed notepaper, from the aristocracy, from Members of Parliament. He had even sent a copy of his booklet to Ronald Reagan, to Mrs Thatcher. I thought he had an adamant vanity.

He left me the story about the fox to read at my leisure so that I could give him an opinion on it when he returned.

As he travelled northwards he phoned me every night.

'I feel,' he said, 'as if you are interested, as if I'm in touch with home.' He discovered the luminousness of landscapes (he himself had been brought up in the city). One night he slept in a barn and when he had asked for a clock to get him up in the morning the farmer had told him, 'You have a clock. You wait.' The clock turned out to be a cockerel. 'Imagine that,' he said. He was happy as a sandboy. Another time he saw a fawn crossing the road.

'Tonight,' he phoned, 'I'm booked into the Caledonian Hotel. I shall pay for my room with some booklets of my poems.' He had already raised the almost unbelievable sum of £2000. 'I ask for cheques so that I won't be tempted to drink the money.'

He also said to me, 'I mentioned your name to the landlady but she had never heard of you.'

Actually it bothered me a little that she had never heard of me. It also seemed to me that my visitor had become more dismissive of me, more sure of himself. After all he was not a very good poet, indeed not a poet at all.

Let me also say that I wished he had not come to the door. I had my own routine. I started writing at nine in the morning and finished at four. He had interrupted my routine and also put me in the position of being hypocritical about his poems. I had met people like him before. For instance, here is a story.

Another poet of approximately the same calibre as my visitor had accosted me once in Glasgow. He was unemployed, his wife had left him, he had smashed his car; his father was dying of a stroke, and his mother of cancer; he had been cut by a razor when he was a bouncer in a night club; he had been charged with sexual assault; he had fallen out of the window of a second storey flat after taking drugs. Now it might be considered that such a person might turn out to be a good poet but in fact his poems were very sentimental and didn't reflect his life at all. Such is the unfairness of literature. What can you do for such people who have experienced the intransigence and randomness of the world and cannot make use of it?

My visitor disturbed me. I imagined him as I have said learning the luminousness of the world, coming across pheasants, foxes, deer; rising on frosty mornings among farm steadings; setting out in the dews of autumn; writing his poems ('I have no difficulty at all: I can write four poems a day easy'); meeting people.

One night he phoned me and said that he was going to have an interview with the Duke of – . The local paper had asked to take a photograph of the two of them together.

Alcoholism is a terrible thing. I know a talented man who is in the entertainment world and who often does not turn up at concerts etc. because he has been inveigled into taking a drink. It was really quite noble that this 'poet' was taking his money in cheques so that he would not be tempted into using it to buy drink. Drily he toiled on, changing his poems and booklets into cheques, having as far as I could see nothing much of his own at all.

I can't write. Isn't that odd? Most days when I sit down at my desk I have no difficulty at all in writing something. But from the time that this poet called on me, I have written nothing. I have dried up. I think of him plodding along a dusty road, stopping at a hotel or a boarding house, negotiating with the sharp-eyed owner, paying for his keep with pamphlets, poems. What a quite extraordinary thing. Nevertheless I should have had nothing to do with him. And I am paying for it now. This is the first time I've ever had writer's block. What does it mean?

Maybe he won't come back. He hasn't phoned so often recently and when he does he sounds more independent, as if the two of us were equals.

Last night he phoned. He had run into another writer in a pub. This writer decorated the wall of his room with rejection slips. He didn't think he was getting fair treatment because he was a Socialist. He dressed in a Wild West outfit. He was 'quite a character'. 'Listen,' I nearly said to my visitor, 'don't be deceived by him. He is a bad writer. I can smell his amateurism a mile away. People like that always dress in an outré manner, they always say that they are not understood. Avoid him. Listen to me instead.'

I started writing when I was about eleven. I believe that routine, hard work is the most important thing in any art. I sit down at my desk every morning at nine. Without a routine all writers and artists are doomed. I have never been an alcoholic. Writing is my life: that must be the case with all artists.

I should have asked him how he had got involved in his walk to raise money for a boy who is dying and is to be sent to America where the 'poet's' wife is. Maybe she left him because he didn't make any money, because he insisted on taking part in such outlandish projects. On the other hand she might have left him when he was in prison. 'They were very good to me in prison. It was there I met the man who illustrated my booklet. I had five hundred printed. Who is your publisher? Do you think you could interest him in my poems, my story about the fox?'

A startling statement he had made was, 'This is all that I have left, my writing.'

When I was younger I actually used to taste the excitement of art. I remember days when myself and my current girl-friend would travel on a green tram in Aberdeen. Mornings were glorious. I used to shout out lines from Shakespearean plays in cemeteries, among the granite. 'The great poet,' I used to say, 'is always on the frontier.'

Later I went back to Aberdeen and had the following fantasy. My earlier self met me on the street wearing a student's cloak. He was with a group of his friends. They passed me in the hard yellow light laughing, and probably never even noticed me. Perhaps they thought of me as a prosperous fat bourgeois. My earlier self didn't recognise me but I knew him. He was as cutting and supercilious as ever.

I don't think my visitor will visit me on his way south. He hasn't phoned for a week now. He is probably lost in admiration for his genuine artistic friend who is so daring. I feel sorry for him. Really he's so innocent with all his talk of cockerels, barns, deer. I am sure he will have another copy of the story of the fox and not ask me for my opinion. Perhaps his companion has heard of me, dismisses me.

Once before my wife left me I saw a small knot of weasels, a mother weasel with her tiny family, crossing the road. They looked like notes in music.

Another thing I have discovered about myself, I hate the cold. And the rain.

Autumn is passing and he hasn't come. I have heard nothing more of him. Perhaps he did after all use some of his money for drinking. Perhaps he has returned to prison. Perhaps he went berserk one night, was arrested. It is not easy to travel alone, and one's wife to be in America. There is no such thing as goodness: aggression must out. The greater the creativity the greater the aggression that is thwarted.

It is winter. There is snow on the ground, he certainly won't come now. And I have not written anything for two months. I begin to write and I fail to continue. The reason my wife left me was that she said I didn't speak enough to her, about ordinary things. As a matter of fact I found that I couldn't speak about ordinary things: I would try to think of something to say but couldn't.

Listen, let me tell you a story which I read in some book or other. There was a mathematician in Cambridge who knew that being over forty he could no longer do original work in his field. So he spent his time making up cricket teams to play against each other. One cricket team would have names beginning with B such as Beethoven, Brahms, Balzac. Another one would have names beginning with A such as Joan of Arc, Aristotle, Archimedes. One day he received a letter from India which contained a number of incomprehensible equations, and he threw the letter into the wastepaper basket. However, in the afternoon he usually went for a walk with a friend of his (also a mathematician) and he told him about the letter and the equations. The result was that they retrieved them from the wastepaper basket. It turned out that they had been created by a young Indian genius who had never been taught orthodox mathematics. He was taken over to Cambridge and died young. It is said that his last words were, Did you notice that the number plate on the ambulance was a perfect cube?

Now I'm sure that man had no small talk.

Who in fact is the boy and what disease is he dying of? Maybe my visitor faked the whole business in order to make money. But no, I don't think so: the story is true. He showed me a newspaper cutting which described the boy but I didn't read it very carefully.

I have difficulty with detail and especially with people's names.

He must by now have collected £3000 with his bad poetry. What an extraordinary thing.

Actually up until the very last moment I didn't believe that my wife would leave me. I used to say to her. You won't find anyone else as interesting as me. She picked up her case and took a bus. And never said another word to me. I waited and waited but she never phoned. I tried to trace her but was unsuccessful. She was quite beautiful: she will find someone.

Actually she used to weep over stories on the TV. She would dab at her eyes or run to the bathroom. At first I didn't realise what was happening.

Every night I gaze up the road before I lock the door. I am waiting for my poet but he never comes. He has become a mythological figure in my mind like the Wandering Jew. His bag is full of undrinkable cheques. His mouth is dry. He cannot afford the money for the phone. All the money that he collects he puts in his bag which swells out like a balloon. Maybe that's it, he can't afford to phone.

   Or he has gone home.

      Or his wife has come back to him.

         Or he has shacked up with his Wild West friend.

            Or he has become so stunned by the beauty of the Highlands that he will never leave them again.

And here I am making money out of his wanderings. By means of this story. Whereas he . . .

I imagine the boy in a hospital in America. He is being watched over by doctors, surgeons. They are all looking at a clock. 'Soon he will come with the money,' they are saying to the boy. 'You must trust him. Till then we can't treat you.' And he swims across the Atlantic with his bag of cheques. He fights waves, he pacifies the ocean with his bad poems. Out of the green water he coins green dollars. And the boy's breathing becomes worse and worse and the doctor says, 'He won't be long now.'

It has begun to snow. He is perhaps out in the snow in the Highlands, perhaps at John O'Groats with his bag. The snow is a white prison round him: he can't even take a nip of whisky. I feel sorry for him. He should come in out of the cold, he has done enough. He has had more courage than me. With his bad poems he has done more than I have with my good ones. I can see that. And he was just as poor as me.

My writer's block has persisted. I think I am finished as a writer.

The snow is falling very gently. A ghost tree clasps the real tree like a bridegroom with a bride. They have had the worst winter in Florida in living memory.

What a sky of stars. And yet I see them as if I was a spectator. I'd better shut the door, he'll never come, my muse in her girl's dress will never come again. I shall have to take account of that.

I heard a story today about a villager. He has run away with a woman much younger than himself and left his wife. It is said that he was the last person anyone would have expected to have done anything like that. What does he hope to gain? What energy, what a strange leap. Will there not come a time when he will make a third spring and then a fourth one? As if Romeo and Juliet were still alive . . .

Last night I thought I saw him emerging out of the snow with his bag. When I went to the cat's dish there was a snail eating the food. Unless I take my bag on my shoulders I shall never write again. Unless I am willing to accept the risk of bad poems.

The phone rang but it was a wrong number.

Imagine first of all surviving in girl's clothes and then in bad poems.

I am sure that when the spring comes he will be happier. I can almost hear the ice breaking, the sound of running waters, the cry of the cockerel. The fox shakes itself out of its prison of snow. Meagre and thin. It laps at the fresh water. All around it is the snow with its white undamaged pages.

Questions and thinking points

1 The subject of this story – the travelling poet's adverse impact on a writer – is simple enough. The telling of the

story is deceptively accessible, but a complex network of themes lies behind it. Vanity, achievement, loss, creativity, suffering, entrapment; consider how each of these applies to the travelling poet, the narrator and his wife.

2 What is the effect of the first person narration, and phrases like 'Let me also say . . . ', 'here is a story . . . ', 'Listen, let me tell you . . . '? Imagine the story told in the third person – why would this not work? (You might find it useful to consider this question in relation to 'two fragments', p. 79, as well.)

Now read what Iain Crichton Smith writes about 'The Travelling Poet':

> This was a complete gift from the world. Everything about the travelling poet is true. He did come to the house, he was in fact travelling to collect money. Or he said he was. He did keep in touch. He did write awful poems and short stories. However, I did make some changes. In reality my wife was there. In the story I am unmarried. The reason I made the change was to emphasise the loneliness of the narrator. In reality I did not suffer writer's block at all. In the story I did because I wished to emphasise the travelling poet's daring in relying on chance to look after him. Thus it is that even with reality one makes changes in the name of Art. It is not often, however, that so much of a story is given by reality. It was a sort of gift.

3 The importance of reality as a starting point is emphasised by many poets and fiction writers. As is the importance of knowing when to change things for the good of the piece of writing. This is the point at which writers have to separate themselves from their work.

   Bearing this in mind, and the fact that Iain Crichton Smith is also a poet, look again at the ending of this story, from 'Every night I gaze up the road . . . '.

Up until this point, the story has been realistic, following the logic of prose. Now the story lifts into another plane, where the logic of poetry is introduced. This section begins with the phrase 'undrinkable cheques' where the compression of language is a poetic device.

Trace the development of the text into fantasy and images of dreamlike significance. What change in the narrator's attitude is paralleled by this change in the writing?

4 The last paragraph deserves close attention. What happens to the tense? How do the details connect with the rest of the story? How do they operate on a symbolic level? And the freed fox lapping at fresh water? How long can the snow pages remain white and undamaged? Do you think this is an optimistic or a pessimistic ending?

Creative thinking and writing

Prose written by a poet has poetic blood in its veins. Phrases like 'he had an adamant vanity' or 'the luminousness of landscapes' (look up 'adamant' if you're not sure of its essential meaning) reveal a musical ear for language and a precise and poetic perception. This is not something you *learn*, but something you *have*. However, if you find this pleasing, the more you read poetic prose writers, and poetry, the more it may rub off on you.

■ *Change is a useful driving force behind a poem or story. It is gentler than outright conflict and can lead to a more reflective kind of story. Compare, for example, the conflict-driven 'Getting Sent For' (p. 39) with this story, whose pace is altogether slower. You may prefer one to the other, or value both equally for different reasons.*

■ *Try to come up with a change, rather than conflict, story. Someone comes into and passes through your life, leaving you changed forever. Write in the first person and try to avoid major conflict. This is to be an introspective, reflective piece, and you may well find your language will shift into a more poetic plane.*

On himself and his writing

Iain Crichton Smith

> Born in Lewis, I write poems, short stories and novels, in both English and Gaelic. I suppose I have written fifty books altogether. I stay with my wife in Taynuilt, Argyll.
>
> I started writing when I was eleven years old, but for a long period I had to earn my living as a teacher. I retired early from teaching and have been a full-time writer for fifteen years. I am extremely lucky. Not everyone does exactly the job that he always wanted to.

Further reading

You'll find more of Iain Crichton Smith's writing in the following, selected books:

Consider the Lilies (Canongate Classics) – a novel
Listen to the Voice (Canongate Classics) – short stories
Collected Poems (Carcanet Press)

If poetic prose appeals to you, you might also enjoy the following books, and other works by these authors:

James Joyce: *Dubliners* – short stories
Gabriel Garcia Marquez: *Love in the Time of Cholera* – a novel
Laurie Lee: *Cider with Rosie* – an autobiography
William Faulkner: his short stories
J. G. Ballard: *Empire of the Sun* – a novel
Tennessee Williams: *The Collected Stories* or *A Streetcar Named Desire* (a play)

HOLLOW

Elissa Soave

She can't wear jewellery any more
It hurts too much
The gold band forced past lumpy bones
And tinsel hoops crashing crazily against the hollows of her face
Where the flesh should have shielded her.
Her dresses fall dismally down
Like soggy rags hung out to dry
Fluttering and lost
Going where the wind dictates.
She's all scooped out
With nowhere to hide
And no place to be.
No thanks, I just ate the biggest meal
As she covets your heaped-up plate
She's dreaming of hot, buttery scones and creamy pasta
Safe and warm
Like her mother used to make
Mummy!
Jesus, you're so thin
The ultimate compliment, yet it's never enough
She thinks she looks like the one on page twenty-three
Almost
But it's getting so hard now
Her limbs seem like stone.
Heavy and so cold
Even the sunlight has lost its power to animate her.
But she tells herself she's nearly there.
Another few pounds. A couple more inches. Closer. Close.
And a lifetime away.
Still, it'll be worth it
To see his face.

Questions and thinking points

1   The first twelve lines of this poem do not reveal the cause of such thinness. How many possible causes can you come up with?

2   The poem is not located in a specific place. Where might this woman be? Do you get any indication of her age from the first twelve lines? Why has Elissa Soave (pronounced 'swah-vay') constructed the poem in this way? How does the construction affect the impact of the subject-matter on the reader?

3   Show how Elissa Soave exploits both line breaks and sentence length to maximum effect. Consider the two lines starting 'She thinks she looks like . . .' and the two lines beginning 'Another four pounds . . .'

Now read what Elissa Soave writes about 'Hollow':

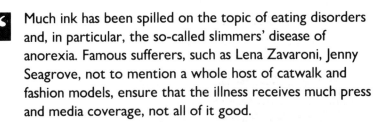 Much ink has been spilled on the topic of eating disorders and, in particular, the so-called slimmers' disease of anorexia. Famous sufferers, such as Lena Zavaroni, Jenny Seagrove, not to mention a whole host of catwalk and fashion models, ensure that the illness receives much press and media coverage, not all of it good.

Perhaps the most frightening statistic about anorexia is that it is increasing rapidly and affecting younger and younger victims, usually (but not always) female. Most people know of someone, be it a friend, a relative, or a neighbour, whose life has been touched in some way by the disease and, more than likely, some of the students reading this poem will, themselves, be able to identify with many aspects of it. At the time of writing the poem, I knew two victims of anorexia, both young girls. I was moved by their suffering, by their never-ending struggle with food, and by their inevitably futile attempts to become thinner, and ever thinner.

'Hollow' is a poem written about anorexia, from the anorexic's viewpoint. When I decided to write the poem, I had at first intended to write *about* a sufferer of the illness. However, as I started to describe the hollow cheeks (which is where the title comes from), the non-existent but still imagined fat, and the way her clothes hung on her skeletal frame, I became aware that, while I was describing the effects of the illness, I was not helping non-sufferers to understand the motives of the anorexic. I added this dimension to the poem by taking snippets of things that had been said to me, and notions that I had read are common threads in the thoughts of many anorexics, and incorporating them into the poem. By thus writing from the anorexic's viewpoint, I felt that I was being more sympathetic to her plight, and less of a voyeur, interested only in the illness's shocking physical effects.

'Hollow' outlines some of the thoughts that pervade the mind of the anorexic, while engaged in her battle with food and weight. She feigns non-interest in food when, in fact, she thinks of little else.

'She's dreaming of hot, buttery scones and creamy pasta' and 'No thanks, I just ate the biggest meal/As she covets your heaped-up plate' illustrate the obsession with food and the devious methods employed to avoid its actual consumption.

Debate has led to numerous theories as to why so many healthy young girls fall prey to anorexia – a desire to stay childlike, and therefore safe ('Mummy!'); intense media pressure to be as thin as the latest catwalk model ('She thinks she looks like the one on page twenty-three'); and the hideous notion that men can only love women who conform to the current media ideal of thinness ('Still, it'll be worth it/To see his face').

Anorexia is a tragedy which our society *must* deal with before it reaches epidemic proportions. Perhaps it is at last time for the girls and women of this world to realise that we are all individuals and we must be loved for who we are, not what we look like.

Advice often given to aspiring writers is that they should write from personal experience, or on subjects that they know about. I agree with this, and feel that the sympathy and sorrow I felt for my two friends helped me to write what I hope is a compassionate and understanding poem.

'Hollow' was written about four years ago now, and, when I read it, I feel sad that so many girls are still going through what 'my' anorexic was suffering in the poem. I am proud of what I have written, and hope to publish some more material related to this subject.

Creative thinking and writing

Elissa Soave draws on emotions as well as facts. Behind these facts lies research, which you, too, can carry out to prepare for a piece of writing. You may well find more than you were looking for. This enquiry process can open up new areas of thought; it can bring you gifts.

■ *Anorexia is only one of many downward spirals in which we can become trapped and which are ultimately self-destructive. Alcohol and nicotine are legalised addictive toxins; others are secret or illegal. Choose an addiction or disorder which you know a little about, researching the subject if necessary. Then try to write a poem about it from an unusual angle which makes the reader see the behaviour in a different light – as Elissa Soave has done.*

On herself and her writing

Elissa Soave

I was born in Scotland on 17 December 1967, and have been writing for as long as I can remember. I started by writing school stories (greatly influenced by the girls' boarding school novels which I used to read voraciously), and typical adventure and mystery stories. However, I soon developed a preference for poetry and started writing poems when I was around 14 or 15.

I studied Law at Strathclyde University, where I won a prize in the Keith Wright Memorial Poetry Competition (under the pseudonym Candice Crystaltips!) and had some poetry published.

I am currently living in Oxfordshire, and studying for a BA Arts Degree at the Open University in my spare time. I continue to write poetry.

Further reading

You can find poems by Elissa Soave in the following anthologies:

New Writing Scotland 8 (Association for Scottish Literary Studies)
Northlight Poetry Review
The Scotia Poetry Competition Prize Winners' Book

SOLITUDE
Helen Lamb

He's a cold child
with a strange old face
and all he wants is
to be warmed
as he slides
his slight shivering form
between our skins.

So solitude lies down.

Wherever we go
he comes too
just slips in between
as if he belongs
and I want to ask
– did you bring him along
or did we create him between us?

Questions and thinking points

1 In the first line, 'cold' is a startling adjective. Explain why
and consider all the connotations of 'cold' – physical and
metaphorical.

2 In the second line, emphasised by its internal rhyme with
'cold', 'old' is again a startling adjective to use to describe a
child's face. Explain why and consider in how many ways the
face can be said to be old.

3 What do you think would happen if this child were to be
warmed up? (Put on your poetically logical hat to answer this
one.)

Now read what Helen Lamb writes about 'Solitude':

 The initial idea for this poem came from a friend who had recently moved to another part of the country. It took him a while to establish a new social circle and, in one letter home, he mentioned his *solitude*. At the time, something about the way he used the word struck me as strange. He'd made it sound as if solitude was his companion – another person almost.

But that wasn't logical, was it? You may or may not enjoy your own company, but in solitude you are definitely on your own. Still, logical or not, somewhere at the back of my mind a contradictory little ghost lingered on. Though it took me a long time to work out who he was.

In fact, the poem wasn't written till many months later and, by then, my friend's letter didn't matter so much. The nature of solitude was what interested me now – the difference between loneliness and being alone, for example. Solitude can be pleasant, after all.

But I was looking for a character to fit the name and an untroubled 'Solitude' wouldn't have been very interesting to write about. It probably took longer to find the right character than it did to write the poem in the end. I wasted a lot of time struggling with dud ideas before I hit upon the child. The problem was that there were so many obvious and clichéd images surrounding solitude and I had to work through them and then discard them before I could come up with a fresh angle.

The child is a symbol, of course. A manifestation of the distance and loneliness that exists between the two adults. But even though he isn't a 'real' child, he still behaves as if he were. Wanting to get into the parents' bed, for example, is a stage most children go through. And, on the surface, this couple with the kid in tow might look like any 'normal' family.

Without the twist, these would be quite ordinary

images and I suppose if I were to offer any advice at all about writing it would be to start with ordinary, everyday situations and let your imagination go to work. You can do a lot with your own experience. You can make it comic, tragic or completely surreal. And big words are not necessarily better either.

Because Solitude is a child, I chose to keep the language simple. No fancy adjectives. The ones used – such as 'old', 'cold', 'strange' – are very basic but, in context, still capable of conveying quite complex meanings, as well as helping to create a stark effect. I also used the layout (with the single line between the two stanzas) to mirror the theme of the poem. So Solitude slips in yet again and this is the only time he's given a name.

4 In the third last line, Helen Lamb writes 'I want to ask . . . ' Why can this question not be asked?

5 Explain the irony in the last line, and the pun on 'between'.

Creative thinking and writing

To think of 'solitude' as a person isn't logical – and a strictly logical mind would stop there, would probably not even reach there in the first place. But in this poem, the creative mind takes over and pushes for a poetic logic.

Helen Lamb talks about the struggle, the 'dud ideas' that she had to work through before she could find the 'fresh angle'. It is comforting to know that others don't always find writing easy. Bernard MacLaverty, too, admits to having written bad poetry. But, for everyone who wants to write, the struggle and the learning processes have to be undergone, and gradually the work becomes a little easier and a little better.

■ *Choose an abstract concept – nothing to do with solitude, loneliness or isolation – perhaps pain, fear, love, hope? See if you can personify this intangible feeling (it needn't take human form; it can be a bird or an animal or whatever you think appropriate) and work it into a poem. Consider, too, whether you find a negative or a positive concept easier to work with. Is fear simpler to characterise than happiness? Will fear lead to a more dramatic character than happiness? Bear in mind that conflict or change is often a productive area.*

On herself and her writing

Helen Lamb

I was born in Stirling in 1956, and now live in Perthshire with my family. I started writing in my thirties and since then my poems and short stories have appeared in many magazines, anthologies (such as *Scottish Short Stories*) and on Radio 4.

Further reading

You can find more of Helen Lamb's work in the following anthologies:

Original Prints 2 & 4 (Polygon)
Fresh Oceans (Stramullion)
Three Kinds of Kissing (HarperCollins)
The Laughing Playmate (HarperCollins)
Meantime (Polygon)

A WEE TATTY

Alison Kermack

He goat the idea offy the telly. Heard oan the news this Chinese boy hud ritten 2000 characters oan a singul grainy rice. Well o coarse, he kidny rite Chinese an he dooted if thur wiz any rice in the hoose (unless mebby in the chinky cartons fi last nite). Butty liked the idea. Whit wi the asbestos fi wurk damajin his lungs an him oan the invalidity an that. Well. He hudda loatty time tay himsel an no much munny ti day anyhin wi it. Anny didny reckon he hud long tay go noo. It wid be nice, yi ken, jist tay day sumhin tay leeve sumhin behind that peepul wid mebby notice. Jist a wee thing.

So wunce the bairnz wur offty skule an the wife wiz offty wurk, he cleared the kitchin table an hud a luke in the cubburds. Rite enuff, nay rice. He foond sum tattys but. Thottyd better scrub thum furst so he did. Then took thum back tay the table. He picked the smollist wun soze it wizny like he wiz cheatin too much, anny began tay rite oan it wi a byro.

He stied ther aw day. Kept on gawn, rackiniz brains an straynin tay keepiz hand fi shaykin. Efter 7 oors o solid con-sen-tray-shun, he ran ooty space. Heed manijd tay rite 258 swayr wurds oan the wee tatty. He sat back tay huv a luke. Even tho heed scrubd it, it wiz still a bit durty-lukin an it wiz that fully ize yi kidny see the rytin very well. Bit still. He felt heed acheeved sumhin. He wiz fuckn nackert. He laydiz heed doon oan the table an fella sleep. He didny wake up.

When his wife goat back fi hur wurk, she foond the boady lyin it the table. She gret a wee bit but theyd bin expectin it. She pickt him up an, strugglin under the wait, tryd tay shiftim inty the back bedroom. Haff way throo it goat tay much furrur an she hud tay leevim in the loabby til she goat a naybur tay helpur.

Wunce she goatim throo the back, she sat doon it the table an thot aboot how tay tell the bairnz. Mebby efter thur tea. Aw kryst, haff foar, she better pit the tea oan. Thursday so thur wizny much in the hoose. She noticed the tattys oan the table an thot it wiz nice o hur man tay scrub thum furrur. She chopped thum up an pit thum oan tay bile.

That nite, even tho the bairnz didny notice, the tiny drop o ink made the stovyz tayst that wee bit diffrint.

Questions and thinking points

1 This story is written in the vernacular. The spelling makes the reader pronounce the words in a particular way. Can you find examples of both syntax and vocabulary which also set the language apart from Standard English? Do you find this writing style off-putting or refreshing? Examine closely the reasons for your reaction.

2 Death and bequeathal (in the form of calligraphic crafting) are two of the themes in this story. How does Alison Kermack set up each of these in the first paragraph?

3 How does the man's achievement differ from the Chinese boy's?

4 Why do the characters have no names?

5 This story is blackly comic. What are the humorous elements? (Consider both plot and language.)

6 The man is dead, leaving a widow and children. His legacy to posterity has been inadvertently destroyed. Why is this blackly comic as opposed to tragic?

Now read what Alison Kermack writes about 'A Wee Tatty':

❝ This is actually one of the first stories I ever wrote. I always wanted to write short stories, seeing as how they're one of my favourite things to read, but I just found it so HARD! I still do. I get to the end of the first page and read it over and go crikey what a load of rubbish! and after doing that about sixteen times I give up. I think the problem with stories is, I read other folk's stuff and think hey excellent! and I want to be that good too. I forget that like anything else it takes a heck of a lot of practice to be as good as the best people. In fact it's a pure fluke that this one turned out halfways decent considering I'd never finished a story before. I've certainly written a lot worse stories since although looking at this one now, I don't think it's that great either: there's not much in the way of character development, and the bit at the end where the point of view changes to the wife, I don't like that (even though it's kind of unavoidable under the circumstances).

Anyway, the way it all came about was, I was lying in my bed one night, just kind of dozing off, and for some reason I minded this thing my wee brother Andy had said to me. He was telling me exactly what it says at the beginning of the story – something he'd heard on the news, the Chinese guy writing all that stuff on the grain of rice – and he said, imagine if his wife had went and bunged it in with the rest of the rice for their tea. So there was me in my bed and I just thought hey, maybe I could make a story out of that, so I sat up right then and wrote the whole thing out, pretty much the way it is now. Of course I never had the whole thing in my head to begin with, just what my brother had said to me, and the rest kind of happened as I went along. I maybe changed a couple of things later on as well, not much but. Usually if I have to change a lot in a story I know it isn't going to work, you know, like if I have to keep rewriting big chunks of it. The best ones just happen naturally, mostly if it's an idea I've had for a long time. I think that's part of the writing process for me, thinking over things for a couple of weeks before I write anything at all. I don't mean sitting down and thinking, I just mean when I'm at my work or in the pub or whatever, and things that folk say or something on the telly or something that happens when I'm at the shops'll maybe give me another idea for a different part of the story and eventually I'll get really excited about it and that's when I'll start writing. It doesn't always work out even then, but when it does it makes all the other times worth it.

Creative thinking and writing

■ *Alison Kermack dislikes the change in point of view from the husband to the wife. Were you conscious of this when you read the story? Why do you think a single viewpoint might be preferable in a short story?*

■ *There's a mischievous mind behind this story which has obviously had a lot of fun writing the piece. Alison Kermack keeps her story very plausible, which adds to the effectiveness.*

See if you can write a blackly comic piece. Think of an essentially tragic situation, perhaps involving death, loss or destruction. You can stray into the realms of the absurd if you wish, but watch that your story doesn't become too fanciful. There are very human emotions and reactions in Alison Kermack's story with which we can all identify.

On herself and her writing

Alison Kermack

I've been writing pretty much ever since I could write. Not all the time, of course, maybe about one poem a month, something like that. Then about three years back I started getting published. I got dead excited then and was writing like crazy, maybe three or four poems and one short story a week. A lot of them were total dross mind you, and it didn't last long either. I'm pretty much back to the one-a-month game by now, not even that at the moment. I used to worry a lot about not writing. There's that much pressure to be 'successful', to get published, get on the telly, all that stuff, and I've never been very career minded about writing so it was kind of hard. I had to ask myself what I was bothering writing for at all if I couldn't make a living out of it and I wasn't worried about how many folk actually read my stuff. I decided I'm doing it for pretty selfish reasons really. It's just 'cause I like it. More than that even – I NEED to write. It's the whole thing of creating something. Of sitting back and looking at something and saying I made that, and it's all right!

Further reading

You can find poems by Alison Kermack in the following book:

Writing Like a Bastard (Rebel Inc. Publications, 1993)

She has also contributed work to the following anthologies:

Original Prints 4 (Polygon, 1992)
Dream State (Polygon, 1994)
Tongue In Yer Heid (B & W, 1994)

THE SEDATED
Gordon Meade

Sedation makes them
Easier to handle, calms them down.
They glide across the ward's
Polished floor carrying their shelled heads
Like snails with hangovers.

Their eyes are sunken
Pools. They don't know what time
Of day it is, what month,
What year. Their cotton-wool brains have been
Saturated with chloroform,

Their threadbare veins
Burnt clear with morphia. At night,
The nurses bring a medicine
Cabinet round the ward on wheels. A dozen
Plastic cups, a dozen cures.

Their mouths close on
The holy tablets. Sleeping, they feel
No pain. In their dreams, they
Are circus performers – tumblers, acrobats,
And clowns. They wake up
With their heads in the lions' mouths.

Questions and thinking points

1 Gordon Meade exploits line breaks several times in the first and
last verses of this poem. In each case the following line spins the
meaning around. Identify as many examples as you can.

2 Line breaks are used for a different effect in the second and third verses – 'They don't know . . . with morphia.' Comment on the effect here.

3 'Snails . . . ', 'cotton-wool brains . . . ', 'threadbare veins . . . ', 'holy tablets . . . ' – comment on the appropriateness of the levels of meaning in these images.

4 Why do you think Gordon Meade chose circus performers as images in the last verse? What is the full significance of the final image?

Now read what Gordon Meade writes about 'The Sedated':

'The Sedated' is one of a number of 'hospital poems' that appeared in my first full-length collection, *Singing Seals*. The poems, as a whole, deal with a period of time I spent in hospital recovering from a fairly serious head injury. As with the other poems set in hospital, 'The Sedated' was written about three years after the events it recalls, and tries to recreate the atmosphere of one of the wards in which I stayed, and the feelings that the time I spent there aroused in me.

'The Sedated' itself came reasonably quickly to me, growing quite naturally from both the initial rhythms of the first two lines and the first image of the patients gliding ' . . . across the ward's/Polished floor carrying their shelled heads/Like snails with hangovers'. The real 'gift', for me, was the final image of the dreaming patients as 'circus performers' waking up to an unchanged, uncured reality, 'With their heads in the lions' mouths.'

As with most of my poems, any revision of 'The Sedated' was hopefully true to both the original impulse and inspiration, and the first draft that, however awkward, attempted to give the experience shape and form. For me, revision is a means not to add anything new to the original, but to hone it down, polish it up a little, and, especially with the 'hospital poems', make a very personal set of experiences more accessible to the general reader.

Almost ten years after its completion, 'The Sedated' is still a poem I incorporate in my readings, as I hope that the atmosphere of bewilderment, and the wish for an escape, no matter how spurious and temporary, still come over as strongly as they did when I wrote the poem.

Creative thinking and writing

Gordon Meade talks of two creative processes – honing the poem down and trying to make very personal experiences accessible to others. The first is craft – working words until they reach their best. Very often this means changing, reducing, compressing and removing. In a poem, every word should pull its weight and, if it doesn't, it ought to go.

The second process, and one which Elissa Soave also mentions, is communication – opening out personal experiences and reaching across to readers. In your work, don't simply record events, as you might in a diary where all you think about is yourself. Instead, think about your readers, too.

■ *Gordon Meade's poem is about an altered state of mind caused by heavy sedation. Various drugs (including narcotic painkillers, anaesthetics and alcohol), as well as strong emotions, both good and bad, can produce an altered state of mind. Either from personal experience, or from close observation of others, see if you can record the changes produced. Think about behaviour, movement, speech, attitudes, reactions and other relevant characteristics.*

Then see if you can find suitable images – no snails or circuses allowed. Now craft the piece into either a poem or a short prose portrait.

On himself and his writing

Gordon Meade

❝ I was born in 1957 and educated at the Universities of Dundee and Newcastle. Although I tried to write poems from the age of about seventeen, I suppose any serious attempt began during my recovery from the head injury I mentioned previously. I feel that I learned a lot about metaphor from the mistakes I made while undertaking a course of speech therapy in London. When asked to identify, from a line drawing or photograph, say, a dog, my answers would range from cat, to log, to wolf, i.e. from opposites to similarities in either sound or meaning.

I have now been writing for over ten years, and the most prevalent motivation comes from a need to try to make contact with the world around me. In my case, this usually takes the form of poems dealing with the environment of the east coast of Scotland, encompassing both the sea itself and its creatures.

More recently I have been able, through both the Poetry in Schools Scheme, and the posts of Writing Fellow at the Duncan of Jordanstone College of Art and Writer in Residence for Dundee District Libraries, to work with other writers of differing ages and interests which, I hope, has had a positive effect on my own writing. ❞

Further reading

You can find more of Gordon Meade's poetry in the following selected books:

Walking Towards the Sea (Villa Vic Press, 1991)
Singing Seals (Chapman New Writing Series, 1991)
The Scrimshaw Sailor (Chapman Publications, 1995)

SURROGATE
Moira Burgess

'There's someone,' the old woman said, 'who knows exactly what I do and when I do it.'

I was surprised at the way she burst out with it, since of course she didn't know me at all. The two young pregnant mothers ahead of us, with whom we'd been idly discussing the headlines, had just been called, one to each surgery. Now we were alone in the waiting-room; I suppose I was reassuringly on her side of forty, and perhaps even had a good-listener look. She was quite agitated, her shiny knotted hands with the dark liver-spots folding and refolding the tabloid in her lap. 'Cathie, 83, Mugged', the blaring letters spelled.

'What do you mean?' I said, looking concerned. I was really rather interested to hear what she'd say.

For such an old bag of bones she was concise enough. 'There are notes,' she said, 'messages. Always when I'm out. The police won't do anything. They just say it must have been a friend. I tell them there isn't anybody left who would be calling, but I think they think I'm a bit forgetful. I'm seventy-nine, you see.'

'Oh, that's no age,' I said with a smile. 'My mother's over eighty and everybody says she's good for her century.'

'That's nice,' said Miss Jenner in an abstracted way. (I pulled myself up for even thinking of her as Miss Jenner. It wouldn't do if I used her name, when she hadn't given it to me.) 'They're not rude or anything, you know.'

'The police?'

'The notes,' she said a little testily. 'They say, oh, things like *Sorry I missed you*. Or *Will call back*. That worried me for a whole week. And once, *Hope you enjoyed the concert*.'

Her faded eyes held mine as if anyone ought to see the horror of that. I put on a puzzled look.

'I'd *been* at a concert,' she whined. 'Don't you see? How did they know?'

'You must have mentioned it,' I said, 'in a shop, or – or at the bus stop or something.'

'But that means they were standing near me.' Her old hands weren't at all steady. 'Listening . . . I'm almost afraid to open my mouth now.'

You don't say, I thought sarcastically. I said in my mother-soothing voice, 'I wouldn't worry. I'm sure there's nothing in it. You don't get phone-calls, do you?'

'Yes!' she cried, certainly shaking now. 'They never speak. I answer, and the phone goes down. It's got so that I tremble for an hour. I'd have the phone taken out, but I really need it. I have angina, you know.'

'So has my mother,' I said. 'It's a very crippling condition, isn't it?'

'Well, it needn't be,' said Miss Jenner with unexpected spirit. 'If you take your pills and behave sensibly, that is.'

'My mother's must be very bad. She can hardly do anything for herself.'

'Are you sure it's angina?'

'No,' I said, 'but she is.' That had slipped out: there was an unwelcome dawning in her pale-blue eyes. Time to tip the balance a little. 'What I would wonder about those phone-calls, if I were you,' I said, frowning, 'is how the person knows your number.'

'I wonder that too,' she gasped. I thought she was in for an attack right there in the waiting-room. 'I've wondered and wondered – '

'Perhaps a tradesman you've had in?' But apparently she hadn't had even a plumber for years. I could imagine her basement flat, damp-furred wallpaper, crumbling sills. 'The meter-reader? The minister?'

'*The minister?*' That really gave her something to think about: I was afraid I had gone a little too far. But she was a loyal Presbyterian. 'No, no. But my name's on my pension book . . . And I suppose the chemist knows it . . . And there's the voter's roll, they could look up the phone-book from that – '

'You might have been carrying a case with a label on it,' I suggested, 'when you were going on holiday some time.'

That rang a bell. 'Last summer,' she said. 'I'd been ill, and I went to a little convalescent home on the coast. Yes, I remember, I did put a label on my bag. In case it went astray, you know.' She gazed at me, blaming herself, her fingers splayed on her thin old chest. You could almost see the palpitations. 'They must have been on the train! Beside me!'

'Or in the bus shelter,' I said innocently, which of course was how it had been.

Fortunately just then the pregnant ladies emerged almost together from the two surgeries, and in a moment the two doctors' lights blinked on.

'I see Dr Fraser,' I said, getting up. 'Look after yourself now, Miss – ?'

'Miss Jenner, Emma Jenner,' said the old idiot, now in such a state that she really didn't know she was telling me.

'Emma,' I said, smiling, 'what a pretty name. My mother's name is Emily, strangely enough.'

I was in the surgery with the door closed before she had tottered half-way across the floor. Her doctor would get an earful today. I settled myself for a chat with Dr Fraser, but I'm sorry to say I didn't get the attention I deserved.

'You're in very good shape for your age, Marina.' Dr Fraser had known me from babyhood and irritatingly still used my flowery and dated first name. When mother died and I moved into a flat of my own, I would call myself Jane. 'What you're describing are tension signs. Do you get enough exercise?'

'I take Mother for her walk in the park every day.'

'How do you sleep?'

'All right, I suppose.' Except that I was constantly in a half-doze in case Mother should call. Just twice in twenty years she had called when I was too sound asleep to hear. 'Marina would sleep through the last trump,' she sweetly informed every friend who came to tea.

Dr Fraser leaned back in his chair and took off his glasses. 'How is your mother?' he said.

'She doesn't seem to keep very well.'

'She hasn't been in to see me, has she? Do you want to make an appointment for her?'

'I don't think she could get to the surgery, doctor.'

'Marina, you pass by here on your way to the park.'

I came out with that argument unresolved and a prescription for more tranquillisers. I thought I could hear Miss Jenner's breathy little voice from the second surgery. Worth hanging about in the chemist's, you never knew what you might learn; and sure enough she came fluttering along in a few minutes with a prescription in her tiny claw. We laughed and exclaimed at meeting up again so soon.

'More pills,' she apologised.

'Mine shouldn't be long.' It would be nearly as long as hers, since I'd handed it over the counter as I saw her cross the road from the doctor's. 'I'm just looking for a hot-water bottle while I wait.'

Choosing that, and belatedly remembering toothpaste, kept me in the shop until Miss Jenner was stowing her bottle of pills in her handbag. We came out together into the windy, fresh spring day. Long ago at university I had joined the hillwalking club. I had stood on the tops three or four times, seeing the quilted mountains stretch north and west. Then Mother had found out, and the idea of me in such danger had brought on her first heart-attack. Today I wouldn't stand on a hilltop in the cold sweet breeze. I would go home to our too-big, musty house, and Mother would complain that I'd been away a long time.

'Which way do you go, Miss Jenner?'

'Up to Thornhill, dear. It's not far away, only I have to take it slowly nowadays.'

'I'm just over the hill. Do let me carry your shopping-bag.'

'That's really kind of you, dear,'

We toiled up the hill. 'Marina, is that you? You've been nearly an hour! Where have you been?' Miss Jenner's patient bent head bobbed away below my shoulder, blue felt hat, neatly rolled white hair. 'I don't think you realise, Marina, what it's like for me sitting here alone. What if the phone should ring? What if somebody tried the door?' My flat, when she died, would be on the crest of a hill, fronting the westerly breeze. 'Please shut that window, Marina. You know about my back.'

Miss Jenner, panting, asked humbly if she might stop for a rest. 'You seemed to be walking a little more quickly there, dear.' I stopped. The fresh breeze fell calm. I stood in the dull heavy street with an old woman, as always, by my side.

'Here we are, dear.'

There wasn't a soul to be seen in the peeling terrace of bedsitter houses. The other side of the street was a run-down play-park with dogs' dirt trampled into the shabby grass. I carried her shopping-bag down the basement steps and stood like a dutiful daughter while her uncertain fingers turned three keys. I leaned forward to put the bag inside the door. There were four more steps, rather steep, leading down into the greasy little kitchen with its old green gas cooker and its stone sink.

'Thank you so much, dear,' said Miss Jenner, setting her shaky foot on the top step. 'Perhaps I'll see you again.'

'Perhaps,' I said.

It only took one push, and as her head struck the corner of the sink there was one hard thud. People would take it for the slamming of a car door. 'Goodbye now,' I cheerfully said. I closed the door firmly so that the lock clicked, and went back home to Mother.

Questions and thinking points

1 What does 'surrogate' mean? Look it up if you're not completely certain. Why is this an ironically effective title?

2 Moira Burgess has crafted this story, setting up the ending right from the opening sentence. Go back over the first six paragraphs and identify the details which now, because you've read the whole story, have additional significance. At what point do you find the first hint of something sinister?

3 How is this element intensified as the story progresses?

4 What can you deduce about the relationship between the narrator and her mother? Justify your comments.

5 What can you deduce about the relationship between the narrator and yourself, the reader? Consider the effect of lines like 'I put on a puzzled look' or 'Time to tip the balance a little'.

6 To what extent can you sympathise with the narrator? Where do you draw the line and why?

7 There are moments of black humour in this story. What, if anything, did you find grimly comical? How is this humour similar to, and different from, that in Alison Kermack's 'A Wee Tatty' (p. 118)?

Now read what Moira Burgess writes about 'Surrogate':

' Unusually, I know where this story came from. I've kept a 'writer's notebook' for many years, and in January 1959 I noted a sentence overheard in the butcher's queue: 'So there's somebody who knows exactly what I do and when I do it . . . ' This was the germ which became an idea which developed into the story. A mere twenty-five years later these words turned up, virtually unchanged, as the opening sentence of 'Surrogate'.

At that early stage I knew hardly anything about how the story would go. 'Persecution complex? Or actual persecution?' I wrote in my notebook. As you see, I must have decided that the speaker wasn't imagining things. More interestingly, I seem to have meant to write the story from the viewpoint of the frightened old woman. At some point over the years, as the idea simmered in my head, I have reversed the viewpoint. The final version is written from the persecutor's point of view, and has, I think, more depth and originality because of that.

Where the mother/daughter theme came from I don't exactly know. There's always a kind of tension between mother and daughter, between childhood love and security and adult independence. As a young adult you can resent your mother and declare you'd happily kill her (sorry about that, Mum). But actually kill her? No. Unthinkable, says the child you used to be. That's the emotional conflict behind Marina's actions.

Marina's position in the story, at home caring for her

mother, isn't one I've ever been in. Unlike her, I left the nest quite early, for work and, later, marriage. My own mother was, however, in her eighties when I wrote 'Surrogate' (though hale, hearty and undemanding), and several of my friends were by then coping with cantankerous, aged parents. Some, like Marina, had never broken away. I suppose I wondered how I'd cope in this situation. (Not awfully well, would seem to be the answer here.)

This 'what if . . . ?' is so often where a story really begins to take shape. And at some point 'what if I – ?' becomes 'what if she – ?' It's a mysterious shift in attitude which the writer doesn't consciously bring about, but which has to happen if a story is going to be any good at all. Out of some of my thoughts, some of my friends' experiences, an overheard remark twenty-five years ago, comes somebody called Marina, not me nor anyone I know, but a separate person whom I can discuss in this way.

Creative thinking and writing

■ *Watching and listening to other people can be fascinating. Observation can also be used as a catalyst for a creative piece, particularly when you ask yourself 'what if . . . ?' See if you can catch a catalyst today. Listen for intriguing fragments and see if you can develop them, through 'what ifs . . . ?' into a story.*

■ *There is always the risk that an unsympathetic main character (in this case a murderer who takes out her bitter resentment of her mother on an innocent substitute) will alienate your reader. Moira Burgess addresses this problem by creating a narrator who takes the reader into her confidence. See if you can come up with an unpleasant character who plots and commits a crime – not matricide. By allowing your narrator to take the reader into his or her confidence, try to write a story that doesn't alienate the reader.*

On herself and her writing

Moira Burgess

> I was born in Campbeltown, Argyll, and now live in Glasgow. I wrote my first story at the age of six and haven't really stopped writing since; working up an idea until it becomes a story is the most satisfying thing I know. Creative writing – novels and short stories – is what I enjoy most, but I have also edited short story anthologies, compiled a bibliography of Glasgow fiction and written a series of local history books.

Further reading

The Day Before Tomorrow (Collins, 1971) – a novel
A Rumour of Strangers (Collins, 1987) – a novel

Short stories by Moira Burgess can be found in the following selected anthologies:

Original Prints (Polygon, 1985)
Streets of Gold (Mainstream Publishing, 1989)
The Red Hog of Colima (Collins, 1989)
The Day I Met The Queen Mother (Association for Scottish Literary Studies, 1990)
Under Cover (Mainstream Publishing, 1993)

If you're interested in reading a book where the narrator is essentially an unconventional, rebellious character who takes the reader into his confidence, try *The Catcher in the Rye* by J. D. Salinger.

SECOND INFANCY
David Kinloch

'We've washed her' said the nurse.
And then we met a bank of sour carbolic air,
My grandmother hovering in a tiny wicker basket,
A gossamer mesh of rib and hair
Caught on its interstices.

Suddenly I remembered that trip with her
To Greenock, the smack she gave me
For imprinting a ring of muck around my eye
When I pressed it to whorls in the pier,
Trying to see the sea.

And later, on the boat, as I pulled towards me
Her cat's-cradle, the game that always made
The shape of her forgiveness,
She kissed me, as I kiss her now.

Looking down through the criss-cross cot,
She seems to gently see-saw
As we did once on disused gangways,
And in the evening light threaded
Between the latticework I briefly see,
Cold waves through the dark rings of my eyes.

Questions and thinking points

1 The first verse of this poem conveys a feeling of lightness and
 slightness and delicacy. How does the vocabulary contribute
 to this effect? And the sound of the words? And the images
 suggested by them?

2 What is the relationship between grandmother and grandson
in the second verse? How does this change in the third verse?
(If you don't know, find out how to play cat's-cradle. You
need to know this to appreciate the poem fully.) And how, in
the last line of this verse, does the balance of the relationship
tip through time?

3 Analyse in detail all the ways in which the last verse connects
with each of the other three verses.

4 How and why does the tense of the last verse differ from the
others?

5 'Cold waves . . .', 'dark rings . . .' – explain as fully as you
can the poetic logic operating here. (Look at the last line of
the second verse, too.) What are the connotations of 'cold',
'waves' and 'dark rings'?

Now read what David Kinloch writes about 'Second Infancy':

❛ The poem came out of the very last visit to my
grandmother shortly before she died in a nursing home. I
hadn't seen her for some time and was very struck and
moved by how frail she had become. My memories of her
were of a strong, able, rather 'difficult' woman who had
looked after my brother and me on occasional weekends
when my parents escaped from us for a break.

She lived most of her life in Cardross on the coast
between Dumbarton and Helensburgh, so my childhood
visits to her were full of the sounds and sights of the sea
and the River Clyde. In my poem – which I wrote some
two or three years after her death – I tried to recapture
some of the strength and tenderness of the mature
woman which, paradoxically, became even clearer and
stronger in my memory as I gazed at the helpless wisp of
a creature she had become. The wicker cot made me
think of the swaying gangplanks on which we had played
together and that game reminded me of the cat's-cradle

which is really the central image of the poem: something that combines both strength and fragility/frailty.

I also wanted to convey a certain sense of mystery, a feeling of standing at the edge of an abyss. Watching my grandmother hover between life and death was a little like trying to spy the sea through a gap in a pier. The little boy was surrounded by the sea and didn't need to kneel down and squint at it in this way. But he did. And the older boy, well aware of the reality of death, nevertheless found its sense of mystery and infinity powerfully concentrated in the shape of this diminutive old lady.

I wrote this poem some years ago and, since I rarely keep first drafts, I'm afraid my memory of the various stages the poem went through is pretty hazy. Like nearly all my poems, though, it started from a single line which 'fell' onto the page without much need of revision. Thereafter there was some hard graft before I felt it was as good as I could get it. Just recently, however, a friend pointed out to me that as I had already played on the homonym sea/see (line 10) earlier in the poem, I really ought to change the last line. I think he's probably right and it now reads as published above. Before this revision, however, the last line read: 'Through the dark rings of my eyes, the sea.' So this goes to show that sometimes it's very helpful to have other people look at your work. Frequently they notice obvious things the author initially overlooks, perhaps because he or she is so close to the experience being written about.

How do I feel about the poem now? It scarcely does justice to the enormity of the event described. Watching somebody you care for dying is a disturbing and humbling experience that stays with you for a long time. Eventually I found words and wove a pattern around that experience, using them to try to make sense of my grandmother's death by relating it to life, to the times we had been together. But I feel really that all our attempts to 'make sense' of such experience are doomed from the start. For me, the moment of silence that follows the poem when I read it out loud (and all my poems are written to be read aloud) is perhaps the most eloquent of all.

6 Why is the current last line significantly more resonant than the previous one?

Creative thinking and writing

It is important (and David Kinloch highlights this) to recognise that critical appraisal from others can be invaluable. It may not be enough to leave your work aside for a while in order to acquire the objectivity you need to appraise it. Another sympathetic mind can be very helpful – but only make changes if you yourself believe they will be for the better. Use your own value system as the basis for any decision you take.

The seas, rivers, lochs, firths and voes are an important part of our world. They can arouse all kinds of feelings, memories and associations. Write a reflective piece on a stretch of water which holds particular significance for you. It can be a poem or an autobiographical piece or a short story.

On himself and his writing

David Kinloch

> I was born in 1959 in Glasgow and was educated there, graduating from Glasgow University in 1982. After that I spent four years doing research for a further degree in French at Balliol College, Oxford. During this time I lived for two years in Paris and I return there often to see friends and generally enjoy myself. Since then I've taught French in Swansea and Salford and am now based at the University of Strathclyde in Glasgow.
>
> I started to write when I was about 12 or 13. I had been ill and was very bored by the period of convalescence imposed by the doctor. I'd just found out that my maternal grandfather had been a poet and so I decided to see if I could write a poem too. I started by trying to describe the furniture in my bedroom in as interesting and accurate a way as possible. That was my first poem. What I enjoyed about that experience is still part of what I enjoy about writing today: the opportunity to transform reality; to give it, through language, an extra dimension; to draw other people's attention to what might too easily be overlooked and help them to see it afresh. I also use poems to comment politically on things that matter to me: recently, for example, I've written a lot of poems about the Aids crisis.

Further reading

Paris-Forfar (Polygon, 1994) – poems

There are many books in which water plays an important part. If you like this topic, then you might enjoy the following:

The Silver Darlings by Neil Gunn
The Old Man and the Sea by Ernest Hemingway

THE APPLE GHOST
John Glenday

A musty smell of dampness filled the room
Where wrinkled green and yellow apples lay
On folded pages from an August newspaper.

She said:
'My husband brought them in, you understand,
Only a week or two before he died.
He never had much truck with waste, and
I can't bring myself to throw them out.
He passed away so soon . . .'

I understood then how the wonky kitchen door,
And the old Austin, settling upon its
Softened tyres in the wooden shed,
Were paying homage to the absence of his quiet hands.

In the late afternoon, I opened
Shallow cupboards where the sunlight leaned on
Shelf over shelf of apples, weightless with decay.
Beneath them, sheets of faded wallpaper
Showed ponies prancing through a summer field.
This must have been the only daughter's room
Before she left for good.

I did not sleep well.

The old woman told me over breakfast
How the boards were sprung in that upper hall;
But I knew I had heard his footsteps in the night,
As he dragged his wasted body to the attic room
Where the angles of the roof slide through the walls,

And the fruit lay blighted by his helpless gaze.
I knew besides that, had I crossed to the window
On the rug of moonlight,
I would have seen him down in the frosted garden,
Trying to hang the fruit back on the tree.

Questions and thinking points

1 Which details make the first verse of this poem sensually vivid?

2 Look again at the description of the old Austin. How does the sound of the words connect with the meaning?

3 How is the idea of slanting and crossing over used on both a literal and a metaphorical level throughout the poem?

4 This poem has an obvious chronological progression – from daytime and late afternoon, to night-time and then breakfast. In what deeper sense is time also a theme of the poem? (Consider the effect the passing of time has on both objects and people.)

5 What colours do you find at the end of the poem? What has happened to the earlier colours in the poem? Why is this so appropriate?

6 This poem has a powerful final image. What kind of a ghost is he? How much fear is there behind the poem?

Now read what John Glenday writes about 'The Apple Ghost':

❝ My wife and I had gone up to visit my mother-in-law, who lived in an old Georgian house. It was my first visit there and I was struck by how run-down most of the house was. We talked for a while, and conversation included my wife's father, who had died some three years before. I had never met him. He had been in the Air Force and was a bit of a Mr Fixit. The house was missing him. That night we were to sleep on the top floor, where there are two identical rooms connected by a little landing. In the other room, my mother-in-law had laid out apples on most of the available surfaces. They were past their best. Our bed was small and cold and uncomfortable so I woke frequently during the night. As I lay awake I could smell the apples in the next room.

The poem came fairly easily after that. It was almost a given poem; most of the ingredients were presented to me on a shelf, so to speak. I embellished and changed here and there. The old woman's words are invented – in the poem I make out that the man is fairly recently dead. I put a fictitious car in the empty garage and lined the shallow cupboards with scraps of wallpaper that would suit a young girl because I wanted to introduce that feeling of the slowly fragmenting family, which, like the house itself, and the car, gently settled after the daughter grew up and left home. The 'shallow cupboards' were actually in my own grandfather's house. My real interest was in the dead man. I wanted to catch something of the space his absence made in the house. I have always found the marks we leave on the inanimate more informative than anything else. I embellish for effect, like Emily Dickinson, telling 'all the truth but tell it slant', or as Don Paterson once said of his own work: 'not true, but truthful' – I found it interesting that my wife and her sisters recognised their dead father in the poem.

As I say, most of the poem came out pretty much complete, though I revised through perhaps a dozen or so reworkings, which for me is remarkably few. Most of my poems are rewritten or retyped umpteen times, each changed word, each omission, demanding a balancing change at another point in the work. I also throw words away as I go, as in sculpture where the finished work lifts out of the waste. Sometimes it's the lines I like best which need to go. At each stage, I read the poem out loud, in an empty room. That way, the faults tend to show up in the breath. As with all my work, I look back on the poem now with a vague dissatisfaction. There are sections I would like to change, but it's too late. The clay is hard. I've moved on to other considerations now and I can't go back.

In the very first draft of the last section of the poem, I worked towards the image I had thought of first: the dead man trying to hang apples on a tree in midwinter. The work was to build a poem that was founded on this line.

The poem is still close to prose at this stage, and indeed there are prose jottings after the last line of this first draft, where I recorded various different strands of thought. I also condense, so that the descriptions given by my wife: 'a kind, quiet man' is incorporated into '. . . his quiet hands'.

Creative thinking and writing

■ *John Glenday likens writing poetry to sculpture; other writers in this book have used the image of honing or refinement. What image do you have in your head of the creative writing process? And if you don't have one, think about it, visualise it. Hunt for the image until you find it.*

■ *'His quiet hands . . .' and 'the rug of moonlight . . .' are both examples of poetic compression, where the meaning is multiplied by the removal of words.*

Try an exercise in poetic compression. Think of a descriptive sentence, such as: 'There are roses growing all over the wall.' Now compress it and see what happens. You may find that it leaps like a wet frog from your hands, as the meaning becomes slippery: 'the rose wall'. We now have a wall with roses, a wall of roses and a rose-coloured wall; maybe a tennis player, maybe a barrier of love or to love. Gifts!

Try writing some sentences of your own and then see if they lend themselves to this volatile technique. It can work wonders, but, if one sentence is going nowhere, don't give up. Try another. And another.

On himself and his writing

John Glenday

' I was born in Monifieth, Angus, in 1952. I studied English
Literature at the University of Edinburgh, but dropped
out after two years to become a van driver. I now work
as a drugs counsellor in Dundee.

I began writing serious poems at the age of twelve and
poems seriously at the age of thirty, when for the first
time I joined a writing class. Here I was encouraged to
read my work aloud, to think about my audience and to

revise (and revise). My first book, *The Apple Ghost*, was published by Peterloo Press in 1989 and subsequently won a Scottish Arts Council Book Award. A second book is scheduled for publication in 1995. I was the 1990/91 Scottish Canadian Exchange Fellow, based at the University of Alberta, Edmonton.

Further reading

The Apple Ghost and Other Poems (Peterloo Poets, 1989)

You'll also find poems by John Glenday in the following anthologies:

An Anthology of New Scottish Poetry and Prose (Third Eye Centre, 1989)
Twenty of the Best: A Galliard Anthology of Contemporary Scottish Poetry (Galliard, 1990)
The Faber Book of Twentieth Century Scottish Poetry (Faber and Faber, 1992)

SCARAB
Ian Rankin

'Take it off.'

The Egyptian was grinning, the grin highlighting his several gold teeth.

'Take it off,' he repeated.

For as long as she could remember, Lily Devereux had worn around her neck that tiny black scarab given to her by her father, and now she was being urged to remove it, in the face of a far greater stone scarab by the sacred lake at Karnak.

'Go on, Lily,' her husband said, while the small Egyptian danced in front of them, his arms shaking.

The heat was appalling, and she wished she were back inside the cool, pillared hall of the temple, instead of out here beneath the bare, blistering sun, wilting beside a biologically dead lake and the huge stone representation of a scarab.

'My father told me never to take this off.'

They had come here to Egypt, actually, for sentimental reasons. Lily's parents had been fervid Egyptologists, and she herself had been born inside the tomb of Seti the First. Ronald and she were to visit that tomb tomorrow, walking in the dust of her violent and bloody birth of forty years before.

In the Cairo Museum they had seen many exhibits which had been excavated by her parents back in the dangerous years just after the war. In Luxor they stayed at the same shabbily genteel hotel where Lily's parents had honeymooned. And now, at the Temple of Karnak, Lily was being enticed to walk three times, backwards, round a smooth, sculpted symbol of fertility.

'But why do I need to remove my necklace?'

The gold-toothed local giggled.

'It is unlucky is why,' he said. 'Stone scarab lucky. Make you to have baby. But black scarab,' he pointed to her pendant, almost daring, it seemed, to touch it, 'not so lucky. Make you not have baby. Is well known fact that I tell you.' He eyed her more closely. 'You have children?'

Lily stared towards her husband. His face was ashen in the heat. She knew that he would rather have been holidaying on the wet, warm coastline of Scotland. Well, of course Ronald and she had wanted children, and they had tried for them. They still tried, though more stoically now on his part, and less tearfully on hers.

Lily took the black scarab from around her neck.

'It's unlucky you say?'

The man nodded vigorously. She placed the scarab in Ronald's hand.

'Backwards three times?' she said.

The man nodded again, giggling. Some other tourists nearby laughed too, enjoying the spectacle and thankful to be bystanders and not participants.

Back in their hotel room, Lily sat in front of the portable electric fan and stared at her fine gold chain with its tiny black charm. She stroked her denuded throat, pushing the scarab about the bedside-table as though probing to see if there were life still in the insect.

Ronald added slices of lemon and ice-cubes to a jug of tonic water. He stared out across the balcony, over the great slow Nile itself with its barely moving feluccas, towards the dry yellow hills beyond. Those hills had once contained the ancient lineage of Egypt, the Kings, Queens, and High Priests, and there Lily had been born, in candle-light and in the eternal coolness of Seti's tomb.

'Surely,' Ronald said now, turning with her drink in his hand, 'surely your father would have known, wouldn't he? I mean, he could hardly *not* have known.'

His face had returned to its natural ruddy hue. He looked down on the scarab in disgust and fear.

'We can easily check up on it,' said Lily. 'But after all, we only have that horrid little man's word for it.'

'And the word of his friends.'

'Yes.' She picked up the black scarab, bringer of infertility, bringer of a twenty-year agony. It could not be true.

'Ronald,' she said, 'hold me, please.'

★

Patrick and Celia Gambon had returned to the Valley of the Kings in 1947 to make copies of the many rows of hieroglyphs and cartouches which, even then, were showing signs of rapid deterioration. They were recognised as experts in this field, and had been talked into making the trip even though Celia was seven months' pregnant when they set out from Geneva.

They travelled downriver from Cairo in the company of Hamdi Hammam, the young man in charge of the workings in the Valley. He lightened the trip through his insistence that they drink special infusions of tea and herbs, whose recipe had been passed down through the generations from his ancestor Paneb, High Priest of Thebes. These infusions would restore their already flagging strength and cool their bodies, while also serving as an aid to the expectant mother. Hamdi fussed so much that the Gambons were forced to conclude that they were enjoying themselves, and they set to work on the copying the morning after their arrival at Luxor.

It was decided that they should work in the afternoons, the hottest part of the day. Thus they could enjoy the cold air of the tombs, leaving the warm mornings and evenings free. Soon, however, they began to labour well into the night, hoping that the work might be finished in good time for them to travel back to Cairo for the delivery of Celia's baby. They found that the oil lamps made the atmosphere of the long, narrow tombs unbreathable, and so worked by candle-light, carefully copying each row of the kingdom's history onto long sheets of rough, thick paper.

Most of the other workers in the valley were dismissed at sundown, but Hamdi insisted on staying on with his two guests. He did not tell them that he was worried about the possibility of their being surprised by the many looters who still searched the valley at night, seeking out undiscovered tombs with their only-too-imaginable riches.

Hamdi sat in silence on a broken slab in the tomb of Seti the First, not daring to disturb the meticulous work of the copyists. One error could mean some future misinterpretation of an entire period in the Pharaohs' history. For Hamdi, that responsibility was too much to bear. He went outside to smoke one of his loosely-packed cigarettes, its red tip and the faint glow from the cavern warning trespassers that officials were still here, guarding the tombs even into the chilled night.

A camp had been set up at the other end of the valley, and there, Hamdi knew, tea and food awaited them, but still his friends worked on. He stubbed out another cigarette and scraped a fingernail over his gold tooth. The immense walls of the valley seemed about to swallow him in his insignificance. He was about to cry out at them, when he heard the first low moan from the tomb of Seti the First as Celia Gambon went into labour.

The two men, anxious as they were, could do little but let the screams, the terrible archings of her back, and the rocking of her head take their ultimate course. Patrick wiped the hair back from Celia's brow and rubbed her hand, calming her with words. Hamdi, spellbound and horrified, could only mutter that there should be women present to help with the labour. Why had he not thought of that sooner? There should be women; this was no place for a man. Looking around, he saw that he was in Seti's frigid tomb, not the bustling adobe house of his imagination, and he giggled. Patrick looked at him accusingly, and Hamdi's eyes obediently drifted towards the floor, where two cockroaches wandered slowly in a mating-circle.

At one point, perhaps hours later, following a particularly intimidating cry, several men ran into the tomb. They carried oil-lamps and wore grimy *galabeas* of thick, pale cotton. Hamdi knew them at once for prospective tomb-robbers, but he was thankful all the same for their company, for their shared language and shared beliefs. He greeted them, and they squatted on the floor of the tomb, passing round cigarettes and waiting for that which must happen. Even Patrick Gambon accepted a cigarette, though he had never smoked before. He smiled in thanks, hurrying back to his wife's side.

Hamdi respectfully kept his back to his old friends while conversing with his new ones, but the other men strained to see what was happening at the end of the passage, making crude jokes and enjoying thoroughly this unexpected turn of events.

Many years later, his mouth full of tarnished gold teeth, Hamdi would swear that he heard the child cry before anyone else. It was a whispered affirmation, quickly replaced by the more audible and recognisable sounds of that first shock of life. Hamdi blessed the baby under his breath, and stood up. Hearing a brittle noise under his foot, he looked down and saw that he had crushed a cockroach as large as a mouse. Through a haze of candle-light and cigarette smoke, he saw Patrick Gambon coming towards him, holding the still unclean child in his hands.

'She's dead,' he said, his voice strained to a whisper, but still finding an echo in the gallery.

At first, Hamdi thought the man must be mad; the child was quite certainly alive. But then he realised that the mother, unused to childbirth, had lost her life in the creation of another. He translated this news to the looters, who murmured their regrets and their prayers. Hamdi held his breath, still thinking of the cockroach at his feet.

One of the small knot of men stepped forward, holding out something to Patrick Gambon. He spoke a few words and Hamdi realised that the man's gift was authentic, doubtless stolen from some uncharted tomb.

'He says that this is a charm, Mister Gambon, and that if worn by a woman it . . . '

'Yes, Hamdi, I can see what it is.' Patrick Gambon stared at the child in his arms. He swallowed and, cradling his daughter, reached out with the palm of his hand for the tiny black scarab.

'Thank you,' he said. *'Shok'ran.'*

The man, bowing and smiling, went back to his friends, who were rising to leave. They called out goodbye, but the man and child were already stalking off towards the end of the tomb. Hamdi looked around him, suddenly alone, a finger touching his gold tooth, and saw the fine paintings on the walls, their colouring still alive after a thousand years of silent ingress. They had survived, he knew now, because they were not important to this life.

Ronald Devereux smoked for the first time in his life as he sat in the waiting-room of the hospital. He rose occasionally to pace the floor, checking from the window that Edinburgh was still Edinburgh outside. He thought again, with some horror, that he was too old to make a good father, too old and lifeless, his heart unsteady after years of thankless pounding and surging, now when he needed it most.

He hoped Lily was all right. It was a miracle, after all, and the doctors explained that at her age it would not be an easy birth. That Egyptian with the gold teeth had been right after all. It was a miracle. But why was it taking so long? He stubbed out his fourth cigarette, a taste like bad water in his mouth. A nurse pushed open the door.

Questions and thinking points

1 If you don't already know, find out what a scarab is and why it's a symbol of fertility.

2 Ian Rankin weaves several symbols into this story. What do they represent? In addition to the scarabs, consider the following: Hamdi's gold teeth, the smoking of cigarettes, the cockroaches.

3 Look at the structure of this story and examine (a) how Ian Rankin interconnects past and present in the first two sections; (b) how the third section differs; (c) the effect this has on the final section.

4 In 'Scarab', the reader has access to 'privileged' information that is not available to the characters: Patrick Gambon doesn't know about the cockroaches, neither Hamdi nor Lily realises the connection between the two of them, nor does Ronald realise – at the end – that he's reproducing Patrick's nervous reaction. What impact does your 'knowledge' have on your relationship to the characters? Look at the confidences that Marina extends to the reader in Moira Burgess's 'Surrogate' (p. 129). How do the two stories compare?

5 What do you think happens at the end of the story? Justify
your decision.

Now read what Ian Rankin writes about 'Scarab':

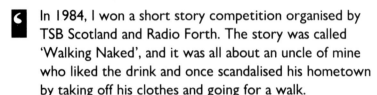

In 1984, I won a short story competition organised by
TSB Scotland and Radio Forth. The story was called
'Walking Naked', and it was all about an uncle of mine
who liked the drink and once scandalised his hometown
by taking off his clothes and going for a walk.

I remember I was horrified when I won, because I
suddenly realised not only that the story would be
published *and* broadcast on the radio, but that all my
family would be listening. I made sure I wasn't around the
night the story was on Radio Forth. My auntie didn't talk
to me for months after.

Anyway, I went to the TSB headquarters in Edinburgh
for the prize-giving. It was during the Festival, and they
got Peter Ustinov to present the awards. I got a
Caithness bowl and £200. The bowl stayed in its gift box,
but the money was something else. I used it to pay for a
trip to Egypt. I had a friend who was teaching English
there, and I fancied a holiday. I went with my girlfriend,
and we flew the cheapest way we could, via Rumania
courtesy of Tarom, the Rumanian air company.

We spent two weeks in Egypt. Sometimes it was great,
sometimes it was horrible. We'd almost no money, no
command of the language, and we probably tried to do
too much. We took a train south from Alexandria to
Luxor, and stayed there a few days. We wanted to visit
the Valley of the Kings, where a lot of the Pharaohs were
buried. Tutankhamun's tomb was still there, along with
other tombs which had been emptied by looters. We
went there by bicycle, not being able to afford a bus or a
taxi. It was a blazing hot day, and we were nearly fainting
when we finally climbed up into the hills.

But inside the tombs, it was dark and cool. We sat

there for ages, staring at the hieroglyphs on the walls. Then we went to a café, and were so exhausted we didn't mind the huge black beetles which crawled across the floor.

It wasn't, however, till we were back in the UK that these experiences and images began to form themselves into a pattern, a sort of story. Tarom had lost all my luggage on the return flight, so I was stuck in London waiting for it. And with time on my hands, I started to jot down ideas for stories based on our trip. I remembered those beetles. You saw drawings of them on the tomb walls. You saw the real things crawling across café floors. And at some ruins near Aswan, we'd been shown a huge stone scarab, the sacred beetle, and the guide had told us that if a woman walked around the stone scarab, she'd become pregnant. Ach, I'd tried to explain to the guide that that's not how babies were made, but my Eygptian wasn't up to it . . .

So I wrote 'Scarab'. Except that I twisted the facts around, inventing a scarab which could make women infertile. My diary tells me that I wrote the first draft in four days, and took another week of rewrites before I was happy with the piece. I remember I used to be very shy about showing people my stories. I mean, I could show them to writers, but I didn't like my friends knowing I wrote them. I was afraid they'd think I was 'soft', or just wouldn't understand the impulse to write.

See, I'd always written. Between the ages of five and ten, I made up wee comic books, with stick characters and speech bubbles. Then I got to like pop music and wrote song lyrics, making up the tunes in my head. And the lyrics rhymed, so they became poems, and the poems were telling stories, so they stretched out and became short stories . . . and now I'd had a story published. And all my friends *knew* I was a writer. So there was no point pretending. I showed 'Scarab' to some friends, and they made suggestions. So I changed a few things before I sent it off. There was this annual collection of stories by Scottish writers, and I'd sent things to it, and they'd always been rejected. But they took 'Scarab', and I felt I was really on my way. I was a writer. I couldn't think of being anything else.

Ten years on, I still can't. Only, I don't write stories like 'Scarab' any more. Somewhere along the line, I started writing crime novels, detective stories. And now I do it for a living, not just because I want to. 'Scarab' seems a long time ago. Writers are terrible: we invent people, give them names and faces and lives. Then we throw them away. It was nice to read 'Scarab' again, and to find those characters I'd forgotten about. And I'm glad I left the ending open. I still don't know what the nurse says when she walks through that door . . .

Creative thinking and writing

■ *Ian Rankin talks of twisting facts and inventing. What is the difference between lying and fiction writing?*

■ *A symbol can add another layer of complexity to a story. There are symbols in our culture which need no explanation – a thistle, a white dove, a black cat. There are other, more obscure ones and then there are the ones you are going to invent! Come up with a symbol of your own. What is it, and what does it represent? Try to weave it into a story in which it assumes great significance.*

■ *Both Moira Burgess and Ian Rankin refer to notebooks and diaries. A notebook or diary, in which you jot down your thoughts and experiences, can be a valuable insurance against poverty of ideas. These jottings are not hampered by crafting or by the thought that someone else might see them. They represent free expression of yourself and perhaps sow seeds of future writing.*

■ *Ian Rankin refers to being shy about showing his writing to his friends. Why do you think this is? Are you happy to show your work to your friends? What is it about admitting you are a writer or a poet that might stop you from opening your mouth? What effect do you think this reticence can have on your work?*

On himself and his writing

Ian Rankin

❝ I was born in Cardenden, Fife, in 1960. I started writing
while still at school, and used some of my poems as lyrics
when I sang in a punk band. When I went to university, I
started writing short stories, until one story turned out
quite long, so I kept with it until it became a novel. It was

a comedy set in a Highland hotel, and was never published.

My second novel, *The Flood*, was published by Polygon Books, which at that time was run by Edinburgh University students. Then a London publisher wanted my third novel. I became a full-time novelist in 1990. Before that, I'd worked in a tax office, on a vineyard, as a secretary and as a hi-fi journalist. I'd published seven books before I was making enough money to write full-time.

In 1987, I published a novel featuring an Edinburgh detective. People kept asking when they were going to see him again. So I wrote a second Inspector Rebus novel, and a third . . . And now I write a Rebus novel every year. But when I get fed up of him, I use a pseudonym and publish other, different books.

Further reading

Recent novels by Ian Rankin include the following:

Strip Jack (Orion Books)
Black Book (Orion Books)
Mortal Causes (Orion Books)

And under the pseudonym of Jack Harvey:

Witch Hunt (Headline)
Bleeding Hearts (Headline)

THE SCOTTISH NATIONAL CUSHION SURVEY
Robert Crawford

Our heritage of Scottish cushions is dying.
Teams of careful young people on training schemes
Arrived through a government incentive, counting
Every cushion. In Saltcoats, through frosty Lanark.
They even searched round Callanish
For any they'd missed. There are no more Scottish cushions
Lamented the papers. Photographs appeared
Of the last cushion found in Gaeldom.
Silk cushions, pin cushions, pulpit cushions.
We must preserve our inheritance.
So the museums were built: The Palace of Cushions, the
   National
Museum of Soft Seating, and life went on elsewhere
Outside Scotland. The final Addendum was published
Of *Omnes Pulvini Caledonii.*
Drama documentaries. A chapter closed.
And silently in Glasgow quick hands began
Angrily making cushions.

Questions and thinking points

1 How do you react to the first line of this poem?

2 Do you know what Callanish is, or where it is? Find out, if you don't.

3 Which single line sums up the message of this poem? How might your reaction to question 2 justify this message?

4 What feelings does this poem arouse in you?

Now read what Robert Crawford writes about 'The Scottish National Cushion Survey':

 'The Scottish National Cushion Survey' was written around 1984 when I was living in Oxford; six years later it appeared as part of my first collection of poems, *A Scottish Assembly.* I've been trying to find the drafts of the poem, without luck, but I know that almost all my poems go through a number of drafts, and I can see from others written around this time, many of which were never published, that I was trying hard to steal effects I admired in the work of the American poet John Ashbery, whose writing fascinated me then and whom I invited to Oxford in 1985. Probably 'The Scottish National Cushion Survey' is a bit better than other fledgling poems I wrote around then because it owes less to Ashbery, though I suspect its pick'n'mix approach to language owes something to his liberating love of a wide, impure spectrum of diction. So I put phrases like 'government incentive' and 'training schemes' in the same poem as the made-up Latin *Omnes Pulvini Caledonii* (which means *All the Scottish Cushions*). I was fascinated by the way Ashbery seemed to be able to take both feet off the ground in a poem and just float with language, but my poems – not least because a lot of them around this time had a Scottish political anchor fitted – always kept at least one foot solidly on the tarmac. Working in Oxford in the Thatcher years, I felt frustrated by how little people there seemed to bother about Scotland. I also felt both annoyed and amused by the way so many folk around me failed to realise the cultural energy that was on the loose in Glasgow. At the same time, though, I was thinking about the elegiac strain in so much Scottish culture, the lament-note that sometimes tends to elegise the living out of existence. All that's a rather intellectualised, after-the-fact analysis that may distort the poem a bit to make it fit a neat grid. Certainly, like many poems, it grew from a combination of gut feelings and intellectual speculations. I wanted it to be funny, yet to have a quality of determined bite to it, creeping round received views and expectations. Using cushions rather than something more predictable was a way of doing that. Looking back, I see that this was also a more traditionally 'feminine' image that I chose, to control some of the more bullish resentment that could topple the poem into crude, macho Scottish chauvinism.

In writing, I was aware of institutions like 'Scottish National Party', 'National Gallery of Scotland', and 'Scottish National Dictionary', and I bounced from there. Also, at the back of my mind were some hand-sewn individual embroidered pew cushions I'd seen at Iona Abbey. Perhaps ideas about sewing and embroidery not being taken seriously (by men at least) as an art form became blended with my concern with Scotland being treated as hardly significant in Oxford.

5 Robert Crawford describes this poem as having 'a Scottish political anchor fitted'. What do you think this means? (To help you consider this, you might find it useful to look back at what G. F. Dutton says about Art and preaching, p. 90.)

6 In both this poem and Edwin Morgan's 'Little Blue Blue' (p. 32), the poet is playing with ideas and language, rather than dealing with the emotion of personal relationships or experiences. How has the form and content of each poem been affected by its purpose?

Creative thinking and writing

■ *Sometimes an oblique view of a situation or an issue can make a point more effectively. It can also lead to humour. If you find yourself frustrated or enraged by something, don't jump up and down, but stand back and take a 'slanting' look at it. And see if you can channel your energy into a creative solution.*

Think of an everyday household object – but not a cushion –

which we all take for granted. Imagine that it's an endangered species. Let your mind run free and make lots of notes on all probable and improbable consequences of this loss. Then write a tongue-in-cheek article or poem about this disaster, finally suggesting a way of turning the tide.

On himself and his writing

Robert Crawford

I was born in 1959 near Glasgow, and grew up there.
Now I work as Lecturer in Modern Scottish Literature at
St Andrews University. I've been writing for as long as I
can remember. Words are our subtlest technology and

our most intimately human asset. The fun of them is as natural, and as uniquely human, as laughter. Poetry, however serious, is language at play. For me, to refuse to read or write poetry would be as perverse as to refuse ever to laugh.

Further reading

You can find more poems by Robert Crawford in the following books:

A Scottish Assembly (Chatto & Windus, 1990)
Sharawaggi, written with W. N. Herbert (Polygon, 1990)
Talkies (Chatto & Windus, 1992)

Robert Crawford has also written and edited several works of literary criticism, of which the following is perhaps the most relevant here:

About Edwin Morgan, co-edited with Hamish Whyte (Edinburgh University Press, 1990)